PRIMITIVES
IN THE
WILDERNESS

PRIMITIVES IN THE WILDERNESS

Deep Ecology and the Missing Human Subject

Peter C. van Wyck

STATE UNIVERSITY OF NEW YORK PRESS

Published by
State University of New York Press, Albany

For information, address State University of New York Press,
State University Plaza, Albany, N.Y., 12246

Production by Cathleen Collins
Marketing by Fran Keneston

Library of Congress Cataloging in Publication Data

Van Wyck, Peter C.
    Primitives in the wilderness : deep ecology and the missing human
subject / Peter C. van Wyck.
        p.   cm.
    Includes bibliographical references and index.
    ISBN 0-7914-3433-8 (alk. paper). — ISBN 0-7914-3434-6 (pbk. :
alk. paper)
        1. Deep ecology—Philosophy.   2. Human ecology—Philosophy.
3. Primitivism.   I. Title.
    GE195.V36   1997
    304.2—dc21   97-3612
                                                              CIP

10 9 8 7 6 5 4 3 2 1

Contents

Acknowledgments   vii

Introduction   1
Whither Environmentalism?   1
Phantom Limbs   2
Methods   5
Structure   9

1. The Move to the Outside   17
   Earth Day I: The View from Space is Better   18
   Reform and Radical   28
   The Social   32
   The Deep   33
   Theoretical Fog   39
   The Minority Tradition   42

2. Ecology/System/Totality   47
   Prosthetic Ecology   47
   State Ecology   51
   Ecology and System   53
   Translation   56
   Ecological Patois   58
   Modernity   62
   Enlightenment   64
   Modernity as Paradigm   69

3. **Displacing the Humans** 75
   Nature Knows Best 75
   The Anthropocentric Circle 79
   Wilderness and the Mirror of the Primitive 82
   Primitive Others 85
   Going over the Hill 92

4. **Boundary Disputes** 103
   Boundary Games 106
   The Cyborg Trope 112
   The Wager 115
   Objectivity and Others 122
   Critical Weakness: Toward a Weak Ecology 127

   Notes 137

   Bibliography 169

   Index 181

Acknowledgments

I wish to thank the following individuals and publishers for granting me permission to reprint selected materials: Donna J. Haraway, "Gender for a Marxist Dictionary: The Sexual Politics of a Word," "A Cyborg Manifesto: Science, Technology, and Socialist-Feminism in the Late Twentieth Century," "Situated Knowledges: The Science Question in Feminism and the Privilege of Partial Perspective," *Simians, Cyborgs, and Women: The Reinvention of Nature.* New York: Routledge. © 1991 Donna J. Haraway. Reprinted by permission of the author. Rosi Braidotti, "Toward a New Nomadism," unpublished manuscript. Holland: University of Utrecht. © 1991 by Rosi Braidotti. Reprinted by permission of the author. Max Oelschlaeger, *The Idea of Wilderness: From Prehistory to the Age of Ecology.* New Haven, Conn.: Yale University Press. © 1991 by Yale University. Reprinted by permission of Yale University Press. Environmental Action, ed. *Earth Day—The Beginning.* New York: Bantam Books. © 1970 by Arno Press. Reprinted by permission of Ayer Company Publishers. Bruno Latour, "An Interview with Bruno Latour." © 1993 by Configurations. Reprinted by permission of Johns Hopkins University Press. Jean Baudrillard, "Modernity." © 1987 by Canadian Journal of Political and Social Theory. Reprinted by permission of Canadian Journal of Political and Social Theory.

Although this work is personal and idiosyncratic, there are a number of individuals that in various ways (which they may or may not realize) have made its present form possible. In particular, I wish to express my gratitude and thanks to Dr. Jonathan Bordo of Cultural

Studies at Trent University. As a teacher, mentor, and friend he has been a singular and profound influence upon my work.

The list is incomplete, but in addition, I want to mention the support and complicity of David Holdsworth, Andrew Wernick, Steven Regoczei, Elizabeth LeRoux, Glenn Macdonald, Keith MacDonald, T. Marks (proof-listener *extraordinaire*), Andra McCartney, Douglas Cohen, Ian McKie, Marike Finlay-de Monchy, Charles Levin, Brian Massumi, Anthony Wilden, Duff Gordon, and my faithful—if machinic—reader, Fred.

I would also like to express my gratitude to SUNY Press, to the valuable insights of the anonymous readers and the patient copyediting of David Hopkins, to the Natural Sciences and Engineering Research Council (NSERC) who made funding available for the early part of this project, and to the Social Science and Humanities Research Council (SSHRC) who have funded my doctoral research.

It is to A. M. A. (presently at large in the "Dark Continent") that I dedicate this book.

Introduction

Whither Environmentalism?

Primitives in the Wilderness: Deep Ecology and the Missing Human Subject is a work of critical exploration. In one sense my principle interest is in the variant of North American environmentalism known as deep ecology. Generally categorized as part of the radical edge of environmentalism, deep ecology attempts to surpass the inherently conservative practices of social and political reform by developing a deeper (i.e., more critical, more robust) understanding of the contemporary ecological problematic. It is, in many respects, seductive. Its promise consists in the realization that there are—for those inclined to listen—minor traditions of thought and practice that may have something relevant to say to those who would speak on behalf of nature. In another sense, though, my interest is to approach deep ecology as an epistemological and discursive field in the interest of discerning the manner in which it retains profound commitments to the very things that it seeks to challenge.

In deep ecology one can see pathological patterns—lines of thought, images, concepts—endemic to environmentalism in general taken to the extreme. By beginning, and remaining, disinclined critically to situate its project against the pervasive and hegemonic flows and forces of modernity (nature/culture, man/woman, male/female, self/other, etc.) deep ecology has been unable to rearrange the conceptual furniture that constitutes our lived world.

I find it both curious and troubling that deep ecology has been so influential, while at the same time remaining so theoretically under-

1

developed. Proclaiming the attempt to situate itself somewhere at the intersection of radical social theory, meta-ethical theory, and the philosophy of nature, deep ecology has, since the early 1980s, revitalized a North American environmental movement that had become compromised, coopted, and disenchanted with political inactivity. By characterizing the dominant or reform stream of environmentalism as *anthropocentric*, ergo "shallow"—and therefore an unwitting accomplice in the dominant values and aspirations of the Western world— deep ecology is intended to offer both a critique and a reformulation of the human/nature relationship in *non*-anthropocentric terms.

The theoretical work that I attempt is to look critically at the foundations of deep ecology, at the conception of the human subject that is advanced within it, and at the very prospects for the human subject in a deep ecological future.

By developing only a superficial and ultimately reactionary analysis of the "modern," deep ecology remains deeply entwined within the very historical forces it attempts to contest. The deep ecological response to the twentieth-century ecological condition is to wish away the harmful effects of the "modern" by imagining a story wherein modern humans have strayed from their pristine and ecologically benign roots. As a result, deep ecology succumbs to a singular and idealized conception of the human, a conception that closes off the possibility of heterogeneous subjectivities by representing humans as a single ecological category.

Phantom Limbs

In order to undertake this critical exploration of deep ecology, I borrow widely from contemporary social, political, anthropological, and philosophical writings, and together with deep ecological texts I endeavor to orchestrate a critical encounter. An encounter that should perhaps have taken place long ago.

My intention in all of this is more to open up a space wherein it is possible to rethink the terms and meaning of environmentalism than it is to feign a scholarly detachment and set the record straight. Such records, historical or otherwise, are never quite straight to begin with. Meanings, as such, are slippery beasts, and the act of critical interpretation is but the performance of possibility. This, of course, is not news. It amounts—in simplistic terms—to an articulation of a basic poststruc-turalist intuition; systems, whether they be social, political, cultural, or historical, are irreducible to coherent and inclusive structures; there is always an other, a haunting, a ghost in the machine. The intuition (I hesitate to say "discovery") of the irreducibility of systems is minimally a result of a series of displacements. Freud, for example, identifies the three great wounds of Western culture: the Copernican revolution, Darwinian evolution, and his own "discovery" of the unconscious. Foucault points out that the sting of these wounds persists, and infects our very interpretive techniques; symbolic wounds upon phantom limbs.[1] And perhaps the idea of a phantom limb is an appropriate fig-ure to describe the historical conditions and influences under which deep ecology operates. The phantom limb is objectively missing, yet it is also present in that it persists in organizing the region it formerly occu-pied. The phantom limb is at once a reminder, and an impossible promise of a return to wholeness and completion . . . phantom God, phantom Marx, phantom Social, phantom Nature.

In a moment of self-reflection on his intellectual development, Lévi-Strauss situated his decision to pursue anthropology as having been specified by a conjunction of Marxism, psychoanalysis, and geol-ogy.[2] His claim was that anthropology did not simply occur to him as an extension of what he had done previously, but was specified by his motivating trinity of passions. I find this very striking. Beyond being a wonderful description of his anthropology, it may perhaps say some-thing significant about critical thought in general. It is not only that anthropology speaks, but that it is spoken through the telluric move-ments of the earth, through the anonymous movements of countless societies, and through the acts and dispositions of individuals. It is hard to envision an outside from which to operate untouched by the force of such totalized and pervasive antecedents.

To follow this idea, I can recall that Carlos Fuentes once wrote that the death of God resulted in the production of a very large God-shaped hole; not an absence as such, but a zone of traces. And to this, Andrew Wernick has added that a similar hole resulted (following the events of May) from the death of Marx; only this time the rupture was decidedly Marx-shaped—this we could call the second death of God. Gianni Vattimo sums up the first aspect of this as follows: "A secularized culture is not one that has simply left the religious ele-ments of its traditions behind, but one that continues to live them as traces, as hidden and distorted models that are nonetheless profoundly present."[3]

The point is that the more we think and act in the world, the clearer it becomes that thought and its articulation must always operate in and around the variously shaped holes which give account of its historical conditions. What manner of thought is adequate to this task? For me at this point the scene of this problem is populated by many figures. From Vattimo and Borradori to Derrida to Foucault to Baudrillard to Lyotard, Haraway, Lingis, Deleuze, Guattari, Deleuze *and* Guattari.[4] All are in various ways engaging the question of the adequacy of thought, of the constraints upon thought, and of the means by which thought may think itself through history and into the next millennium.

My method is thus to identify these phantom limbs, these covert commitments which—while perhaps not objectively present—persist nonetheless as traces, distortions, presuppositions that are there from the start.

After Deleuze, we could say that part of my approach is to show how the conceptual and theoretical space of deep ecology remains entrenched within an "image of thought" that constrains its potential to say something new. The "image" in this context refers not precisely to ideology, nor is it some formulation of the imaginary—though it is implicated in both. Rather, it is a kind of monster that squats upon thought, weighing down upon it. Images here refers to "a whole organization which effectively trains thought to operate according to the norms of an established order or power, and moreover, installs in it an apparatus of power, sets it up as an apparatus of power itself."[5] It is the foundation at the root of thought, the presuppositions that are there from the start: thought or thinking as an innate capacity or faculty which has an affinity with the true. Under the sign of a common sense, a pre-philosophical ground—image—enters into the procedures of thought.[6] To proceed in thinking in a manner that fails to conform with this image of thought requires a kind of philosophical obstinacy and implies a struggle against the image. The project of thought becomes an attempt to (modestly) not know what *everyone knows*, and (modestly) deny what *everyone recognizes*.[7]

The image of thought to which Deleuze refers could in part be expressed as the transhistorical sway of foundationalism. Many of the authors that I invoke here are engaged in particular fashions with questions concerning foundationalism, and all are engaged with certain antifoundational (or counterfoundational) gambits. Where I become entangled in all of this is precisely at a metatheoretical impasse. Perhaps *impasse* is too strong; yet at each turn I become aware that the practice of theory is fraught with impediments to saying anything new. Well beyond any concern with the tyranny of influence, what gives me difficulty is that theory today is utterly distracted by the conditions of its own possibility. This is by no means any kind of nostalgic lament; more an acknowledgment of the burden to which the task of thought has a responsibility. I struggle with the issue of how to move thinking out of an always already critical mode (a place occupied with both villains and allies), to something active and affirmative. A difficult task, yet a prerequisite it seems to me, to finding a place from which to speak. Yet if, as Deleuze has said, theory really is a toolbox, one may easily err on the side of too few tools (or perhaps too many of similar configuration). The plethora of applications that confront a critical project today simply demands a robust accompaniment of tools. In the language of hardware: if the only thing one has is a hammer, everything must surely become a nail (Nietzsche's philosophical hammer notwithstanding).

Methods

As a kind of transdisciplinary endeavor my intention is to explicitly forge links between the often rarefied zone of theory and the irreducible materiality of culture. In this sense theory is predicated upon an engagement with the world—it *is* practice. For some this practice goes by the name of cultural theory, or cultural studies. Such a field is in part characterized as a set of theoretical and political practices that focus—in the absence of any stable, ahistorical methodology—on questions of social, political, and cultural relations. Aware as I am that to submit questions of political and social practice to definition can often do more harm than good, the following from the introduction to Grossberg, Nelson, and Treichler's *Cultural Studies* is, I think, a thoughtful characterization of the position to which theory must aspire. Cultural studies, they write, is

> never merely a theoretical practice, even when that practice
> incorporates notions of politics, power, and context into its
> analysis. . . . [C]ultural studies offers a bridge between theory

and material culture. . . . In a period of waning enthusiasm
for "pure" and implacably ahistorical theory, cultural studies
demonstrates the social difference theory can make. In cultural studies, the politics of the analysis and the politics of
intellectual work are inseparable. Yet intellectual work is, by
itself, incomplete unless it enters back into the world of cultural and political power and struggle, unless it responds to
the challenges of history. Cultural studies, then, is always
partly driven by the politics of its context and the exigencies
of its institutional situation; critical practice is not only determined by, it is responsible to, its situation. Through the last
two decades when theory has sometimes seemed a decontex-
tualized scene of philosophical speculation, cultural studies
has regularly theorized in response to particular social, historical and material conditions. Its theories have attempted to
connect to real social and political problems.[8]

A bit grand, perhaps. But I think this marks a very contemporary
realization that if theory aspires to gain any kind of significant political
foothold in the world, it must also attend to its own contingencies and
artifice. Since theory must always be produced from some specific location, and from some concrete set of circumstances, to deny its own historical dimensions—its own phantoms—is to engage in a kind of
subterfuge, an intellectual fiction, that pretends theory can be disen-
gaged from the political and social world.

My political engagement in this work is motivated by the sense
that environmentalisms such as deep ecology are in no way adequate to
the task of theorizing—much less acting upon—the complexity of the
contemporary ecological situation. But my disillusionment with respect
to environmentalism is pitted against my equally felt conviction that
something must be done. The theoretical tools to which I appeal do not
afford me a position on the outside of all of this. Nor do they lay claim
to any unquestioned rights and privileges; indeed, such procedures are
minimally about being savvy to such tricks of omnipotence. I adopt the
posture that I do in part because it provides a rich language within
which to pose the sorts of questions I wish to ask, and partly because
such critical practices are, simply put, pleasurable. But beyond all this, I
think it is important to stage a meeting of these domains if only because
they have, largely, remained strangers.

In undertaking this critical work on deep ecology, I hope to accomplish two goals. First of all, I want to bring to bear some of the methodological and theoretical perspectives of "cultural studies" on deep ecology in order to draw out and elucidate some of its theoretical and political shortcomings. There is, to be sure, a language difficulty inherent in this; for the most part cultural studies is discursively a foreign language to deep ecology. This kind of environmentalism, in its desire to find or rediscover the "truth" of humans as ecological beings, has remained mostly isolated from contemporary theoretical debates which have—in the social sciences and humanities, at least—undermined (if not entirely dismantled) the very foundations upon which such truths may be constructed. The domain in which deep ecology has been set out—for the most part—does not acknowledge the matrix of social, cultural, and historical conditions beyond that of its analysis and diagnosis of the current *ecological* condition. It would therefore seem crucial that deep ecology be brought into the view of contemporary social and cultural theory. But just as deep ecology has remained theoretically isolated, cultural studies has not paid a great deal of attention to "environmental" questions.

I think that part of what is being said today is that there *are* social and cultural micro-practices we can look at that do run counter to dominant culture (from independent "zine" production to tree spiking); that there are (albeit often in playful and apparently nonthreatening ways) oppositional lines of force that can be identified. And we have, via de Certeau, Bourdieu, and others, theoretical means for seeing these practices as political or emancipatory endeavors that run counter, somehow, to the hegemonic and increasingly homogeneous North American or Western social existence. We can look at these counterpractices and attribute to them recuperative, and essentially creative political and tactical powers. We can thus see them as sites of resistance. But I will resist the temptation to valorize the writing and practices of deep ecology as practices of resistance. Much as it is interesting to explore and theorize such practices that take place at the margins, it is of equal importance to resist the urge to valorize these practices *qua* marginal. As Lynn Spigel put it, "[i]t seems unproductive . . . to place people on the pedestal of righteous political action, to claim that all popular practices are always oppositional related to the structures of power.[9]

It strikes me that this is an important—if obvious—admonition. In the case of environmentalism—nature fandom—we may have some-

thing that amounts to political action ("righteous" or otherwise) but it
is an entirely open question as to whether or not, and in what ways it
might be oppositional to structures of power; in fact, we could come to
the opposite conclusion.

Thus my second goal is to attempt to see how "cultural studies"
can enhance and extend the discourses of environmentalism. Specifically, my interest here is around questions of the subject and subjectivity. It is my sense that the discourses and representations of
environmentalism (in particular, deep ecology) have been deployed in
such a way as to foreclose any novel debates concerning human agency.
Far from embarking upon discussions of what futures might be worth
living, of what new sorts of subjectivities or politics might be imaginable, and of what new kinships might be discovered between earth-
bound denizens (human and nonhuman, organic and inorganic), these
sorts of discourses tend to privilege a strategy of a return to what was
deemed a premodern condition (posthistoric primitivism, as some like
to call it[10]). Humans, on this account, having strayed from a path of
authenticity and connection, must return to a prior state; a state exemplified by the imagined (and imaginary) existence of the "primitive."
And the place where these "primitives" live, is of course "wilderness"
(a place by definition absent of a modern human presence). What can
amount to a Disneyland meets Mutual of Omaha style of ethnography
threatens real humans with real violence in the name of authenticity
and ecological necessity. It is my contention that there are rich areas of
thought—in the humanities and social sciences—that are entirely relevant to rethinking the "ecological subject" that are simply never offered
entry into the epistemological universe of deep ecology—or indeed,
much of North American radical environmental thought.

It seems clear to me that as the stable, luminous, and knowing subject lapses into historical disrepute (from the slave of Meno, to the
Cartesian cogito), what emerges from the political and philosophical
wreckage is a highly contested and volatile zone of negotiation. Equally, it
seems clear that there has been no clean epistemological break separating
before and after; there are zones of attraction which color and constrain
any and all such negotiations. (It is in this sense that the *post*modern begs
the question.) This marks another dimension of the poststructuralist
problematic: a subject cast adrift from its center, no longer coinciding
entirely with itself. Meaning and truth, predicates upon which a fully
centered subject had access to the world, recede into deferrals and

displacements. Identity—and other rights and privileges accorded to the centered and knowing subject—give way to divided selves, displaced selves, to multiplicities; subjects that never fully coincide with identities.

However radical this particular poststructuralist insight has been, it has all too often been construed as an authorization to somehow reverse the valences of the culture/nature binarism in favor of culture. Such thinking, however, does not particularly advance questions with respect to the subject any more than does a move to subordinate culture to nature as deep ecology attempts. To say, for example, that the body is no longer a natural or biological entity, does not with any force of necessity free bodies from determinations beyond that of a certain biological essentialism. In other words, it may simply move bodies from the organizing efficiency of a biological destining, into a zone of cultural (in)determinations (e.g., radical constructionism). But if we observe that socially enforced norms of behavior, in short, cultural specifications of what *bodies can do*, can be every bit as intolerant and restrictive as biological and anatomical determinisms ever were, the shift to culture loses its emancipatory quality.[11]

All of this to say that I remain as aware of the danger of textualizing the world as I do of naturalizing text. In this, and other senses, I ally myself with such theorists as Donna Haraway and Rosi Braidotti. Their work, I think, manages to remain constantly aware of the seductive imperatives of the thorny poles of nature *and* culture. I attempt to do likewise.

Structure

The outline of this work is quite straightforward. The first three chapters constitute the critical work on deep ecology. The final chapter is an attempt to break open a space in which a non- or less foundational environmentalism might start to make sense. I have made no attempt to be comprehensive. My sole concern has been to track a critical path through deep ecology in the interest of shifting the discussion into a different, more affirmative space. For the reader certain things may appear to be missing. For example, I have not given much consideration to the relations between deep ecology and certain traditions of American literature (typically aligned along the Thoreau-Snyder axis). Apart from the fact that this would have entailed a substantially different work, I have simply opted for an alternative trajectory; a trajectory constituted by the sorts of questions I felt the need to ask.

Chapter 1: The Move to the Outside

I begin this chapter by looking at how North American environmentalism seized upon a number of themes and organizing principles that have subsequently constrained and reduced the possibility of its radical insight. The central transcendental operation that is undertaken in pre–deep-ecological environmentalism (and repeated in deep ecology) is the construction of a holism that attempts to displace modern humans from a role of dominators of nature. This operation—that I will call the *move to the outside*—is discussed in relation to the "Whole Earth" and "Spaceship Earth" metaphors.

The move to the outside accomplishes a reduction in difference at one level, by shifting to a larger, more inclusive category; that is, if the earth is a spaceship, then all humans are terrestrial astronauts, and if the earth is a large (super)organism, then humans are simply organic life. While the move to the outside allows environmentalists the convenience of an epistemological shorthand to speak and conceive of humans as a single, unified category, the enormous reduction in complexity which results has very real and politically undesirable consequences: simply put, political, social, and cultural difference tends to disappear.

Having set out the theoretical trajectory of pre–deep-ecological environmentalism, I describe more specifically the topology of radical and reform environmentalism in order to isolate the distinctive character of deep ecology. Beginning with the founder of deep ecology, Arne Naess, I describe the philosophical basis of deep ecology as it was originally formulated, and from here I move on to a description of how deep ecology has actually been received in North America. The chapter concludes with a consideration of the deep ecological program in North America, and its privileging of the "minority tradition."

Chapter 2: Ecology/System/Totality

With the move to the outside described as providing the foundational inertia, and with a contextualized picture of deep ecology in view, this chapter shifts frames and takes a more oblique and generalized look at deep ecology in terms of its relationships to ecology, systems theory, the Enlightenment, and modernity.

In the first case, I attempt to illustrate the rather complex relationship between ecology and environmentalism. A number of other writers have argued that environmentalism fails the moment it attempts to see the world through the eyes of science (i.e., ecology); that "real" nature vanishes from view and something mute and mechanical appears in its place. I engage this argument both because I think it is essentially misguided, and because it seems to reach its limit in the vilification of science as *the* problem with environmentalism.

I argue that ecology functions in a kind of prosthetic relationship with environmentalism. Deep ecology contends that ecology is more than simply *a perspective* about the world; it tells us that ecology is *the* scientific and natural narrative. But at the same time as deep ecology makes what appears to be an attempt to claim the social authority and legitimating rights and privileges accorded by ecology *qua* science, it simultaneously claims to oppose what it sees as the mechanistic and Cartesian (and, ultimately, violent) assumptions of the scientific project. But as I endeavor to explain, the relationship between deep ecology and ecology is not as simple as a scientific discourse being deployed to buttress and cloak a normative program. As I argue, there is simply no such stable category of "ecology" (scientific or otherwise); indeed, ecology demonstrates what we could call a discursive elasticity that allows it to be used to structure the world in any number of ways. To demonstrate the way that ecology is very much the progeny of both "science" *and* a desire for moral reverence, I give a brief analysis of the normative foundations of general systems theory and its relationship to environmentalism.

The ecology/environmentalism argument thus exhausts itself, and points to other questions. Prominent among these is the (perhaps not so curious) motivation in deep ecology to construct a total account, a metanarrative that describes modern existence as having strayed from the proper course. Deep ecology is in many ways an attempt to "reenchant" the world and to offer minor traditions as avenues for rediscovering primal ways of knowing. This longing for an authentic past, and a rekindling of interest in aboriginal and folk myth and tradition is symptomatic of deep ecology's inability to critically apprehend possible relationships *between* myth and Enlightenment. The relationship to the modern that is cultivated in deep ecology is manifestly reactionary. It is not too difficult, I think, to see a disquieting similarity to the political and social climate of ennui that preceded the rise of National Socialism in Germany. I argue that this reactionary spirit comes about (or is at least fostered by) the tendency to view modernity as both a set of practices that force us to see things in certain ways, *and* as an arbitrary and alterable trajectory for humankind. The conclusion of the chapter focuses on the selective critique of modernity that is undertaken in deep ecological literature; a critique that tends to culminate in a wish to construct a futuristic premodernism. The "postmodern age" is thus taken to provide an opportunity to reconstruct a presumed prior organic unity.

Chapter 3: Displacing the Humans

In this chapter I move away from a relational analysis of deep ecology to look in more detail at how humans figure in the deep ecological picture. How it is, in other words, that living and prior humans are actually represented in deep ecological literature.

The assumption of a prior organic unity (essentially a creation story for deep ecology) sets in motion three constructions: the future primitive, the primitive, and the privileged space that these figures inhabit—"wilderness."

The first construction has to do with living humans, their ecologically derailed relationship to "nature," and the "ecological subject" that stands as an icon of deep ecological consciousness.

The second construction is about the "primitive" and how it is made to stand both as evidence of an ecologically harmonious past, and as a prescriptive template for the future.

The third construction—wilderness—is the place where real nature is said to reside. Wilderness is a privileged space for deep ecology, and it is a space that is absent of modern humans.

Through a reading of the constructions of the primitive and its proper place, wilderness, together with the representational practices of deep ecology, I argue that deep ecology can all too easily amount to an ecological colonialism. By ecologizing the world, all other (contesting) discourses tend to get silenced. By remaining unwilling to consider the artifice and foundationalism of its constructions, and by launching a very large and transhistorical move to the outside, deep ecology severely undermines attempts for real living humans to articulate political identities that might not appropriately coincide with the deep ecological *Weltanschauung*.

Contemporary humans and the cultures they inhabit are represented by deep ecology as constituting a fallen state. Seeking to undermine an historical construction of nature as Other, deep ecology comes to represent modern cultures as Other in relation to a prior authenticity. Deep ecology thus emerges as permeated with the very domination that it sought to undermine. Because deep ecology has no adequate theory of politics, history, cultural difference, or the subject, one must conclude that it stands to do far more harm than any good it could accomplish. That is, to confront the diversity of human endeavor by denying its very complexity threatens real humans with real violence.

This chapter concludes the critical work on deep ecology. In the end, deep ecology stands much as a cautionary tale of what can happen when good intentions meet with a little bit of philosophy, science, and anthropology. But the traps into which deep ecology has almost unerringly fallen do have something useful to say. In other words, that which constitutes deep ecology's remainder is precisely what must be attended to.

Chapter 4: Boundary Disputes

In the previous chapters I argue that as a vision of an ecological future deep ecology carries within it a great deal of unexamined assumptions. Apart from its theoretical shortcomings, its historical glosses and its idiosyncratic diagnosis of the modern, one could say that the real problem with deep ecology is that it attempts to be *deep*.

The strategy of depth is always one of going beyond, of overcoming, of finding something more fundamental, more essential. Like theology, depth attempts to set the record straight, to replace error with truth, and in so doing, seeks to recover a lost authenticity.

The final chapter amounts to a theoretical excursion. My interest is to direct attention away from the deep ecological subject toward a more general picture of critical practice. It is an attempt to gather together the various bits of critique and extract the critical basis for creative and affirmative conceptions of the future.

I will argue that—as an exemplar of critical practice—the cyborg figurations of Donna Haraway offer more appropriate political, philosophical and strategic grounds for "a patterned vision of how to move and what to fear in the topography of an impossible but all-too-real present, in order to find an absent, but perhaps possible, other present."[12]

I begin with a consideration of the general condition of the boundaries that support and found the deep ecological subject. These boundaries (human-animal, human-machine, and physical-nonphysical), once assumed to be fixed and dependable, today have become sites of considerable and ongoing ideological dispute.

Drawing from the work of Donna Haraway, Alphonso Lingis, Iain Chambers, Gianni Vattimo, and others, I explore the implications of these contemporary boundary disputes, and endeavor to explain how the decline of certitude marks a novel opportunity for humans to become engaged in creative acts of boundary making.

Haraway's figure of the cyborg enters the discussion as a lively, contradictory, and provocative actor that represents a better figure for the future than the salvific principle of the ecological subject.

The cyborg is not at all concerned with being deep. Its origins are complex. And it represents a hybrid of nature and culture. As an artifact of the very boundary breakdowns that produce it, the cyborg has no recourse to a notion of authenticity, or a return to a natural simplicity. It operates by affinity and complicity, not by reform and representation. The cyborg is a figuration of a political praxis that remaps what can count as a political actor or agent.

The theoretical strategy of the cyborg is a redefinition of objectivity and the knowing-subject position of objective disengagement. It is about limits, location and responsibility; that is, situated knowledge. Its strategy can therefore, I argue, be understood through the frame of what Gianni Vattimo has called "weak thought." As a countertradition within contemporary poststructuralism, weak thought takes an alternative approach to the diagnosis of the modern condition. It sees no radical break that would separate "us" from the metaphysical traditions from which we struggle to become disencumbered.

Weak thought is the recognition that the dream of a radical overcoming (of modernity, of history, of the autonomous pretensions of reason) is a response of strength, and thus a response that answers only the demands of the traditions it seeks to contest. Accordingly, strategies of weakness operate under the awareness that no such definitive farewells are possible. Rather, a weak strategy proceeds from the understanding that even with the decline of Truth's certitude, and the decentering of the knowing Cartesian subject, these traditions persist as illnesses, traces, ghosts. The cyborg, we could say, is a performance artist of weak thought.

I conclude with some remarks concerning how the strategy of weakness, a weak ecology, may offer a way out of the impasse of an ecology of depth.

1

The Move to the Outside

As contested zones of meaning, Nature and the environment have moved to the fore in Western political and social thought in the past decades. Under the flag of Ecology, a politics of the environment has been activated. Throughout the development of the contemporary "environmental movement," one can trace both widely divergent, and essentially similar tendencies.

For convenience, and therefore arguably, I shall place the inception of this movement on the occasion of the first Earth Day: April 22, 1970. Certainly one could do this differently. One could choose names rather than dates: Rachel Carson's *Silent Spring*, Aldo Leopold's *Sand County Almanac*, Gilbert White's *The Natural History of Selborne*. However, what draws me to Earth Day is that it is a particular point in time, an event, in which various (and disparate) political and social forces became gathered together and organized around a common set of concepts to do with the Earth.

By isolating a point in time I attempt to raise certain questions concerning the radical environmentalism of deep ecology; questions that are essentially of a philosophical, epistemological, political, and theoretical character. My interest here is not to present a history. My intentions are far less expansive. What I seek to identify here are certain themes and discourses that came to prominence in and around the time of Earth Day that have persisted within radical environmental theory. By working through a discussion of certain important themes and theoretical orientations, I will move toward a more contextualized picture of deep ecology.

17

Earth Day I: The View from Space is Better

One can read certain important themes and tensions, as well as begin to trace the amorphous outline of the early environmental movement within statements made during the Earth Day, 1970 celebration. Many of the following pieces are culled from a hastily compiled volume (Earth Day was in April, the book was published in May) entitled *Earth Day—The Beginning.* Subtitled *A Guide for Survival,* the book proclaims itself as an inauguration of a movement "to reverse our rush to extinction." The problems that it addresses include:

Pollution. Overpopulation. Overkill. Slums.
Racism. Wasted Resources. Planned Obsolescence.
A Widening War.

This brief text is exemplary for a number of reasons. First of all, as a cultural document the book brings to bear an astonishingly diverse range of perspectives upon the significance of a single point in time. Earth Day represents both a beginning and an end; a recognition of a condition, and an imperative for change. Secondly, the editors of the collection (the staff of Environmental Action) have clearly gone to lengths to construct a unity of voice from the fifty-odd contributions that are included. It is a book of its time; the overall picture that emerges is white, male, and middle-class. Women have not been accorded a collective voice; of the five women contributors, none speak explicitly from a feminist perspective on the environment. People of color are given a chapter—Black Survival—that includes a single entry: a transcript of a black street theater piece (but then there is also a chapter entitled "People"). Not a single piece either speaks to or was delivered by a North American aboriginal person. These observations are not about being "correct" in terms of a constituency, but about the kind of self-representation that the environmental movement undertook in 1970.

> *[We] are building a movement, a movement with a broad political base, a movement which transcends political boundaries. It is a movement that values people more than technology, people more than political boundaries and political ideologies, people more than profit. It will be a difficult fight. Earth Day is the beginning.*[1]

This statement captures well the grassroots humanism that was being articulated though the environmental movement. Ironically, the overtly anti- (capital P)Political orientation of this statement echoes the whole social movement *against* political disaffiliation that had been ongoing in the States and elsewhere since the early 1960s. It speaks to a political and social climate that senses a disconnection with itself and with its social and political aspirations.

One can also detect in this statement (and for that matter, within the very idea of an Earth Day as spectacle) the attempt to subsume difference at one level by shifting to a broader, more inclusive category: a totalizing move that I will call the *move to the outside*. This marks a spirit that we might identify as the *"We"* shift.

The We-shift attempts to ground a struggle in a common language; the common language in this case is the language of the "people." But such a shift may end up creating a new and total position. Moving from profits, technology and political ideologies to the level of "all people," ignores the fact that people *are* (in varying degrees and combinations) *about* profits, technology, and political ideologies. "Moving to the outside" can too easily erase the fact of tremendous inequities in the way profits, technology, and political ideologies mediate the lived experience of human subjects. And on another level, moving to the outside shifts attention away from humans as subjects existing in various relations of power, to humans as objects of administrative control.

Consider two other positions that demonstrate a centrifugal tendency toward the outside:

> One view of the future is that no real future exists. Then there is another view of the future which is in a sense what Earth Day is all about. This view suggests calamity lies ahead if we don't stop some of the things we seem to be insistently doing, things like polluting the air, destroying our rivers, killing our oceans, and jamming our cities. Such a view of the future is circular like the whole Earth. A circular future means we cannot escape from whatever we do here and now. Life is not linear, it is round.[2]
>
> We are nearly halfway through the first year of the last decade of life on Earth as we know it. In this decade of the '70s, Western Civilization will choose one of two paths: it will

*stumble onto the path of extinction, or it will find the way to
live in peace with nature and with itself.*[3]

Thematically, these elliptical and apocalyptic assertions reflect several
other dominant issues within the environmental movement of the early
1970s: pollution, population and, most importantly, the earth as a
closed system.

Although often contested, there was a belief that pollution (never
particularly well defined) as a byproduct of industrial and social development was *the* central focus of the environmental movement. This
identification of pollution as both symptom and metaphor comes
largely from the ground-breaking work of Rachel Carson.[4] To a large
extent the focus on pollution was reinforced politically because a claim
against pollution managed to challenge nothing fundamental about
Western life; it simply admonished Western society to be more aware
of industrial and urban externalities. What these statements foreground has less to do with the political and social character of existence, than with its material conditions. The rhetoric of "let's clean up
America for the sake of its future," offers litter-free sidewalks, clean
rivers, and low-density cities as a prescriptive model for the renaturaliz-
ing of Western civilization. The focus on context over content is symptomatic of a conception of environment as being out there, external
and material.

The population problem has been a perennial topic of social criticism since the time of Reverend Thomas Malthus (1766–1843) and his
Essay on the Principle of Population (1798). The xenophobic algebra
of growth that was mapped out by Malthus was rekindled by Paul
Ehrlich in 1968 (*The Population Bomb*).[5] The "Zero Population
Growth" movement constituted a significant voice throughout the
period of the late 1960s and early 1970s. Not surprisingly, the population stream of environmentalism has traditionally contained the most
conservative elements within the movement.

One of the most long-standing heirs to the zero population growth
program is undoubtedly Garrett Hardin.[6] What Hardin accomplished,
in a very influential paper published in 1968 ("The Tragedy of the
Commons"), was to raise a fairly central problem: the growing population of the planet is apparently outstripping "our"—in its fullest irony
and ambiguity—capacity to feed these numbers. Carrying capacity is
given as a real constraint; a planetary structuring principle for produc-

tivity. The logic he points to at the root of this problem—the intrinsic self-interested rationality of individuals—marks the point at which he begins construction of an evolutionary and historical account that casts all manner of subjectively understood categories (e.g., conscience and denial) as sealed in a genetic and Darwinian necessity, and subject to what he sees as the precarious and fickle forces of natural selection. All of this seems to operate in the interest of protecting economic growth via the mechanism of removing consumers (i.e., the genetically undesirable, and [terminally] reproductive *Homo progenitivus*—read, underdeveloped nations). And all of this is in the interest of maintaining economic growth within the limits of carrying capacity. The solution, Hardin says, must be private property and free markets.

The move in this case, the structuring principle of carrying capacity, illustrates clearly a move to the outside. Hardin's conceptual use of carrying capacity accomplishes a shift outward to a planetary scale; the earth becomes a delicate and closed system. This transcendental operation simultaneously utters a death threat—transgression of carrying capacity—and offers a path to escape: privatization of the globe. The earth-as-closed-system image functions discursively as a kind of stamp of causal necessity together with equal amounts of *ye shall reap what you sow* fervor.

In the strong sense of this closed-system metaphor, there is no *out there*; the earth becomes a dangerously overloaded lifeboat containing everyone. The only practical means of exercising control over such a vessel is to fashion a platform on the outside, so to speak, a platform from which administrative control and technological interventions are possible; the move to the outside accomplishes precisely that.

Hardin's carrying capacity is given force by the character of the threat which humans pose. These threats are, properly speaking, ecological. Threats to carrying capacity are total since the concept of carrying capacity itself is an index of the possibility of continued (human) existence. Jonathan Bordo writes that threats of this type must be distinguished from ordinary threats because

> they have the character of threatening or being perceived to threaten the very existence of groups and collectivities where the fate of an individual is inextricably linked to the fate of a larger group and the threat to its survival. They are not the kind that might be enunciated "I will die but I will live on in

my work, my children, through the community." They have both an ontological and a transcendental quality, putting at risk the existence of living entities as wholes. Ecological threats are prototypical threats to standing since they attack the conditions and relations supporting life.[7]

Bordo captures well the manner in which ecological threat must be distinguished from other sorts of threat or risk. However, rather than a claim that such threats are "prototypical," I would say that what distinguishes ecological threats is that they operate both above and below a threshold. Above, in the sense of the transnational and transpolitical character of, for example, Chernobyl. And below, in the sense of threats that operate at or below the level of biology. In the former sense the effect is direct, but simply too large to be dealt with in terms of models of risk and responsibility. And in the latter, the risk is insidious, and even though it may represent a threat to continued life, it is significantly nonlocalizable, and as such is displaced in relation to a victim/perpetrator model.[8] In both movements of ecological threat, there is a convergence on a point that is subsumed by the ontic.

In his analysis of the modern and archaic responses to the prospect of ecological threat, Bordo points to the always "modernist" or foundationalist vision that underlies and constrains. Comparing Sophocles' *Oedipus the King* to the Brundtland Commission report (discussed below), he observes a similar usage of the oracular voice that is displaced from the scene of ecological threat in order to make pronouncements upon it. The only conceivable stance that can oversee the totality of ecological threat requires the construction of a site where such total vision can be secured.

> The modern response to ecological threat summons the organization of the planet into a unitary techno-administrative system. The modern response is to create a unanimity by making an abstractive step to envelope the world into a larger system: worlds become the world, the world becomes the Earth, the Earth a planetary subsystem, and so on.[9]

The "modern" response, then, *is* the move to the outside. Or perhaps better put, the move to the outside is prominent amongst a repertoire of modern responses to ecological threat. The following illustrates this operation via the encompassing metaphor of the "spaceship."

We travel together, passengers on a little spaceship, dependent on its vulnerable reserves of air and soil; all committed for our safety to its security and peace; preserved from annihilation only by the care, the work, and the love we give our fragile craft.[10]

Advanced by theorists such as Kenneth Boulding and Buckminster Fuller, the spaceship metaphor evokes a concept of the world as finite, closed, and mechanical. Reiterated in this case by a Democratic senator, this metaphor demonstrates both its scope, and compatibility with popular political discourse of the time. With this trope, its advocates proposed a variety of spaceship/cybernetic revisions to the political, economic, and social orders. The blend of technological optimism and naturalism implicit in this statement and vision, became and remains an important theme in environmental discourses. The spaceship metaphor marks the total technological colonization of the earth.

This *Whole Earth* rhetorical move that we hear uttered by Mondale marks a curious outlook on technology that sees it, on the one hand, as a discourse of promise, and on the other, as something that if allowed to run its course uninterrupted, will realize its disastrous telos. To intervene in ecological threat by fashioning a techno-spaceship platform for a transcendental viewpoint, or by fixing concepts such as carrying capacity as totalized structuring principles, the intention may be the attempt to redirect the human/technological telos toward a more ecological unfolding. The result, however, is that

> a sort of transcendental holism becomes the thought device for the constitution of a planetary Foucauldian administrative panopticon whose aim it is to integrate the human being into the world, creating a larger and more elaborate system to be orchestrated by the gaze from a transcendental point "from space," a point that is of logical, moral and administrative necessity beyond the world.[11]

This figure of the panopticon which Foucault describes maps quite precisely onto the organizing efficiency of the spaceship metaphor. As Foucault makes clear, the panopticon accomplishes an efficient and efficacious intensification of power via an application of architecture and geometry. The spaceship move marks a panoptic schema transformed into a universalized model of surveillance and control. The major effect of the panopticon is

> to induce in the inmate a state of consciousness and permanent visibility that assures the automatic functioning of power. . . . [T]he Panopticon must not be understood as a dream building: it is the diagram of a mechanism of power reduced to its ideal form; its functioning, abstracted from any obstacle, resistance or friction, must be represented as a pure architectural and optical system: it is in fact a figure of political technology *that may and must* be detached from any particular use.[12]

What is it to assume this kind of position beyond the world, to undertake a move to the outside? From one perspective it is the attempt to structure an arrangement of agent and patient. The move to the outside allows the earth to be organized (as Bordo points out) as "Earth-as-patient." So construed, the earth becomes an object "beneath the distant gaze of the extra-terrestrial observer."[13] Ecological threats can then be viewed and understood through the metaphors of disease. But equally I think the extraterrestrial gaze is a gaze turned everywhere inward, on itself; not just the Earth viewed in a total operation from space, but the Earth becomes simply a transparent point *in* space.

In another and perhaps more general sense, this move to the outside to obtain a position beyond the world reflects the urge to gain a perspective which theorist Donna Haraway describes as a self-fulfilling pretense at objective disengagement. The agent-object binarism

> both guarantees and refreshes the power of the knower, but any status as agent in the productions of knowledge must be denied the object. It—the world—must, in short, be identified as thing, not as agent; it must be a matter for the self-formulation of the only social being in the productions of knowledge, the human knower.[14]

The patient, then, must always retain the status of *object* both in order to permit routine and directed interventions, and to secure for the agent the role of control. The view from space both objectifies, and provides a platform with total vision:

> "From space" the agent can view the Earth as an organismic whole bound together through the inextricable systemic links

of ecological interdependence. The Earth's toxicity falls beneath the extraterrestrial gaze of the polluting agent, the human subject.[15]

Haraway describes this will to objective disengagement as the "God-trick"—the view from nowhere and everywhere; the ultimate objective position. It is the position that has no location; or what amounts to the same, one that has all locations at once. The God-trick, says Haraway, is the "standpoint of the master, the Man, the One God, whose eye produces, appropriates, and orders all difference."[16] Haraway's political analysis tends to engage this problem from the point of view of the subjugated or marginalized. Accordingly, she seeks an account of knowledge production that avoids the distancing operation that constructs a privileged site from which to objectify.

Haraway would likely argue that the Whole Earth metaphor acts as an invitation to participate in the God-trick. But in an important sense it's more than an invitation; it is a promise of an omniscient vision, and a promise to deliver us from history. Both are promises of impossible operations, but both are backed up with an implicit threat of ecological peril. As Haraway points out in reference to such moves, it is a promise of "what they cannot, of course, deliver, or only pretend to deliver at the cost of deathly practices."[17]

The move to the outside can be characterized in yet another (more overtly political) sense; a sense that is implicit in my use of Bordo and Haraway, but worth making clear. In both senses of the move to the outside, through properties of site, stance and structuring, we have critical depictions from the outside in, so to speak. Another question that therefore presents itself is: what becomes of the heterogeneous *inside* when it is recast as an organic totality when under the structuring gaze from an imaginary position on the *outside?*

The question of exactly who is "we" is clearly problematic, and mostly rhetorical. Whether undertaken pragmatically, strategically, politically or ideologically, any conception of "we" is always a fiction constructed to create linkages of sameness. Establishing a "we," creating a community, is both the possibility for collective dissent, and a means for silencing it. The move to the outside is a means for establishing the guise of a community—Gaia, the ecosphere, spaceship Earth—that leaves no possible space for difference; paradoxical, because the only way to have a "we" is to have something that is not "we."

The question of who is constructing the "we," and what differences are being overwritten in order to create a unified category becomes critically charged when faced with the move to the outside. Framing the question this way helps to identify more precisely the stakes that are involved in grounding a struggle on the homogeneous characteristics of a very large constituency. Diverse voices, represented here by Hardin and Mondale, orchestrate moves to the outside that tactically differ, but the outcome remains a central problematic both for the environmental agenda, and for attempts to articulate emancipatory politics (environmental or otherwise).

The "we" in the case of Earth Day was clearly operating from multiple registers:

> *Yes, it's official—the conspiracy against pollution. And we have a simple program—arrest Agnew and smash capitalism. We make only one exception to our pollution stand—everyone should light up a joint and get stoned. . . .*[18]

> *What we are saying is that we are going to pick up the shit in this country, but in a context of a movement to liberate ourselves. . . . We are saying that we will not be coopted for token changes in a system that plunders and rapes and destroys all over the world. We say to Agnew Country that Earth Day is for the sons and daughters of the American Revolution who are going to tear capitalism down and set us free.*[19]

These two statements, from a speech by Rennie Davis (member of the Chicago Seven) speak from the revolutionary edge of the movement at the time. There are two strong currents that one can quite clearly interpret. First, that the question of pollution must be understood in the larger contexts of social change ("black liberation," women's rights, free speech, anti-imperialism), and a critique of capitalism vis-à-vis freedom and the American Revolution. And secondly, the acknowledgment that the political embrace of the pollution issue itself must not be allowed to divert the course of revolutionary practice. This radical left, Yippie environmental discourse, if somewhat prominent in the late 1960s and 1970s, has all but disappeared in North America over the intervening years. Notable exceptions to this—to the heritage of the left, at least—would be Murray Bookchin's social ecology (discussed below), and the socialist ecological critiques of theorists such as William Leiss and Anthony Wilden.[20]

The Vietnam War and the ecological crisis have the same roots. Both are products of a highly technological, mechanistic, dehumanized society; in the one case ruthlessly expanding its interests in southeast Asia, in the other, ruthlessly expanding its interests at home; in the one case, economic imperialism; in the other, ecological imperialism. One can't fight one without the other.[21]

Here is the explicit claim that exploits in Vietnam and the environmental situation in the United States were born of the same impulse. Through making the claim about imperialism as the foundational impulse, or at least the locus for the historical inertia, an attempt is made to make a critical politics *the* agenda for the environmental movement. This passage is perhaps the most interesting; at least insofar as it is the only example of an analysis that identifies a particular kind of relationship between technology and the ecological crisis. In the years following Earth Day, this point comes to mark a fulcrum that would separate radical from mainstream environmentalism; the radical side viewing technology as inextricably linked with domination and alienation, and the mainstream side seeing technology as a benign (if historically misused) tool.

It is appropriate, as we meet on Earth Day, to remember that Man is a messy animal.[22]

Ladies and Gentlemen, let me state at the outset that Ford Motor Company shares your concern over air pollution. We recognize that we have an obligation to help solve the problem and will continue to go all out in attacking the problem— from every practical standpoint—until it is solved.[23]

An apology dressed up as an alibi, and a corporate commitment to undertake *practical* measures. The first, from the secretary of the interior, and the second, from a Ford Motor Company executive. The first, in a sense, facilitating the second. The representative from Ford speaks from the point of view of *solutions*, and reduces the public outcry to "concern over air pollution." Bracketing and reducing the ecological situation into technically solvable elements came to be the avenue by which business and industry could become *ecological* citizens. A brilliant maneuver, really. And one that would allow industry to simultaneously manufacture and conquer a new market—the commodification of pollution.

Clearly, the Earth Day spectacle offered a little something for everyone—from trade unions to Republicans. The entirety of the political and social discursive terrain was open to articulating an environmental position. Environmentalism on Earth Day, 1970, was very much like a neutral platform that could authorize almost any perspective or orientation, while at the same time giving a vague appearance of unanimity; of course there was no discursive unity—what we witness is more on the order of a political maneuver to construct the appearance of agreement.

Reform and Radical

The fragmentary unity organized by Earth Day, poses certain problems if we wish to speak of North American environmentalism as a contemporary social field or phenomenon. We need, in other words, to construct a more precise taxonomy, to delimit the main environmental discourses that lay claim to the term, and to make clear the senses in which it is used.

The distinction that is commonly invoked to delimit trends within environmentalism is between reform and radical environmentalism. This distinction is often deepened on the radical side through the replacement of "environmentalism" by the term "ecologism"; note that ecologism tends not to be used synonymously with environmentalism. The distinction between environmentalism and ecologism was first set out by Murray Bookchin in the early 1960s.

> "Environmentalism" tends increasingly to reflect an instrumentalist sensibility in which nature is viewed as a passive habitat, an agglomeration of external objects and forces, that must be made more serviceable for human use.[24]

On Bookchin's account, Ecologism differs fundamentally from environmentalism. Ecologism, which Bookchin claimed to be coterminous with scientific ecology, deals with a much broader conception of humanity and nature.[25] Ecologism operates with the view that humanity must show conscious respect for the spontaneity of the natural world, a world that is much too complex and variegated to be reduced to simple Galilean physico-mechanical properties.[26]

Bookchin's distinction was meant to delimit an environmental tendency that seeks to discover the roots of contemporary ecological dangers within the realm of the social (hierarchy, domination, oppression). He distinguishes this approach from the kind of environmentalism that

does not bring into question the underlying notion of the present [Western] society that man must dominate nature; rather it seeks to facilitate that domination by developing techniques for diminishing the hazards caused by domination. The very notion of domination is not brought into question.[27]

For the purposes of this particular work I will accept Bookchin's point that there exists some sort of fault line between an overtly instrumentalist environmental position, and some other positions, not entirely instrumental, that we could call, in relational terms, radical. Although it is important to keep in mind that in the past decade or so the simplicity of Bookchin's topology has ceased to be entirely useful. The radical wing of North American environmentalism/ecologism has itself shattered into many lines of opposition. There is now an exceedingly large complex of interests that are not so easily categorized.

The reform stream of environmentalism is taken to operate within and through existing political and social structures in an attempt to effect change on the level of policy, social habits, and perceptions without significantly altering anything fundamental on the level of social, political, or economic relations.

Accordingly, reform environmentalism may be understood as an instrumental means by which to reduce or delay the ecological crisis through technological and administrative intervention. In this sense, ecological problems are problems of accounting. For example, whereas pollution has historically been thought of as an externality, as a component external to the flows of production and exchange, it now becomes an accounting entry such that an *economic* value is attached to it. Reform environmentalism attempts to enact through changes to policy and legislation an increase in the number and scope of environmental and ecological parameters that become internal to present political and economic systems. Thus when air and water are acknowledged to have been damaged or threatened by the externalities of industrial or domestic processes, the problem becomes one of a more responsible, prudent form of management and administration for air and water resources. Reform projects are motivated exercises in an operative form of pragmatism that is founded on the belief that *every problem has a solution*.

An extreme and complex example of a global reform project is The Brundtland Commission report, *Our Common Future*. This report was the work of the World Commission on Environment and Development that was formed by the United Nations in 1983. Ostensibly a blueprint for a threatened planet, the report details (in a manner not unlike a user's guide) a framework for attaining a "sustainable" condition for global development.

> The concept of sustainable development provides a framework for the integration of environment policies and development strategies—the term "development" being used here in its broadest sense. The word is often taken to refer to the process of economic and social change in the Third World. But the integration of environment and development is required in all countries, rich and poor. The pursuit of sustainable development requires changes in the domestic and international policies of every nation.[28]

The report never challenged the notion or ethic of growth, but instead adopts a prudent position in the recognition that environment is a "real" constraint to efficient and continued growth and development. The Brundtland project entailed a planetary rationalization of the environment as a finite resource base:

> we are serving notice—an urgent notice based on the latest and best scientific evidence—that the time has come to secure the resources to sustain this and coming generations.[29]

In reading the Brundtland report, the figure of the panopticon as a mechanism describing the move to the outside gathers force. Foucault's point that the panopticon must be seen as a political technology, apart from any particular application is critical here. Enclosing the planet in a global development scheme (i.e., making the world a safe place for both capitalism and "nature") requires a kind of panoptic efficiency to achieve its result. The point is not that such grand panoptic strategies of reform are simply about a global imposition of capitalism. It is much more subtle than this. Panopticism functions not through despotic control, but through diffusion and lightness, speed and disciplining—in a word, efficiency. It is not a single and focused mechanism of power, it does not organize into a single point of tyranny. Rather it marks a multiplication and diffusion of power such that "the exercise of power is not added on from the outside, like a rigid, heavy constraint, to the functions it invests, but is so subtly present in them as to increase their efficiency by itself increasing its own points of contact."[30]

The diffusion of power, and the disciplining of social bodies that panopticism promised prompted Bentham to see in his newly discovered instrument a tremendous gift to the exercise of government. He proclaimed:

> Morals reformed—health preserved—industry invigorated—instruction diffused—public burdens lightened—Economy seated, as it were, upon a rock—the gordian knot of the Poor Laws not cut, but untied—all by a simple idea in architecture![31]

It is interesting then to compare the claims made for the global structuring of sustainable development in the Brundtland report:

> Revive growth. Change the quality of growth. Conserve and enhance the resource base. Ensure a sustainable level of population. Reorient technology and manage risks. Integrate environment and economics in decision-making. Reform international economic relations. Strengthen international cooperation.[32]

Radical environmentalism is said to take a different view of the contemporary ecological situation. Its critical stance is in explicit opposition to panoptic reform maneuvers such as that exemplified by sustainable development. From the start there is an assumption that present political, social, and economic structures cannot sufficiently conceptualize—much less act upon—the ecological crisis, and, more importantly, that the ecological crisis is in some sense the inevitable result of the design of contemporary society. This position presupposes that in order for Western society to turn the tide of the ecological situation, radical and fundamental changes must take place; not just at the level of social, economic, and political policy, but at the very foundation of the social, economic, and political.

The Social

Within the field of radical environmentalism, both the etiology of the ecological crisis and the strategic interventions envisioned to enact changes in
humankind's mode of living are highly contested. In terms of the political
topography of radical environmentalism, the central axis—that is, fault
line—along which the movement is (very much) divided, delimits two
distinct approaches or orientations: deep ecology, and social ecology.

The central distinction between these two orientations is that
social ecology (variously termed anarcho-communism, eco-anarchism,
left libertarian communitarian green) is committed to the idea that the
ecological crisis is a continuing result of the existence of hierarchy,
domination, and exploitation (economic and otherwise) in all spheres
of social life.

Social ecology, as articulated by Murray Bookchin, is a political,
social, and philosophical program that seeks to address and resolve the
ecological crisis by reharmonizing social relations in all spheres of social
existence.

The exploitation of the natural world as a field of resources is
deemed by social ecology to be the result of historically determined
social relations within capitalism.

With roots in leftist, libertarian, and anarchist traditions, social
ecology is an attempt at a left green perspective. It rejects orthodox
Marxist interpretations of nature (and human nature), and opposes the
idea that humanity

> confronts a hostile "otherness" against which it must oppose
> its own powers of toil and guile before it can rise above the
> "realm of necessity" to a new "realm of freedom."[33]

Bookchin stresses his view that Marx failed to undertake a radical critique of capitalism. In failing to do so, Marx unwittingly constructed a
scientific socialism that functioned as an anticipatory apologia for what
emerged as state capitalism. By not questioning the Enlightenment conception of nature as a field of utility for human conquest, or the social
relations of domination of man over woman, family over child, labor
over freedom, Bookchin contends that Marx unwittingly turned many
features of capitalism into technical features of production.[34] What
Bookchin attempts with his ties to Marx is not a refurbishing, but
rather, that the

simplification of the "social problem" into issues like the restoration of local power, the increasing hatred of bureaucratic control, the silent resistance to manipulation on the everyday level of life hold the only promise of a new "revolutionary subject" on which resistance and eventual revolution can be based.[35]

The social ecology project amounts to mining leftist traditions in order to discover principles and ideals that can adequately construct a philosophy of freedom for the late twentieth century. Bookchin attempts a philosophy that seeks to avoid the reproduction and recapitulation of power relations (inter- and intraspecific) based on hierarchy, conceptions of rationality founded on instrumentalism, while at the same time not divesting itself of what Bookchin sees as the valid achievements of the Enlightenment. For Bookchin this means appeal to anarchist writers such as Peter Kropotkin, the revolutionary gender politics of Louise Michel and Emma Goldman, the communitarian visions of Paul Goodman and Lewis Mumford. What we end up with in social ecology is a left-based, politically libertarian, and communitarian, ecological environmentalism.

The Deep

Unlike social ecology, deep ecology is less concerned with social analysis than it is with defining a new *ethical* relationship between humans and the natural world. The fundamental difference in points of departure of these two streams of radical environmental thought— one based on the human domination of humans, the other based on human domination of nature—has made for a deep and often bitter division within the North American radical environmental scene.[36] The polarity of these two radical positions on environmental theory notwithstanding, deep ecology, perhaps not so oddly, seems to be gaining not losing ground. To simplify matters, from this point on my use of the term "radical environmentalism" will signify that body of thought and aspiration connected with deep ecology and its associated movements; I will for the most part leave aside Bookchin and social ecology (which as a political and natural philosophy is far less problematic).[37]

I have been suggesting that there are a number of conceptual and theoretical difficulties deeply interwoven at a foundational level within the radical environmental movement. I will now briefly address the way in which deep ecology came to occupy a critical space within this movement. Of primary interest will be what we can take as the three important aspects of deep ecology:

Deep ecology as a critique of environmentalism
Deep ecology as a philosophy of nature
Deep ecology as an ideological and political program.

As a system of normative and prescriptive precepts deep ecology (or transpersonal ecology, or foundational ecology) represents a dominant stream of thought within the contemporary environmental movement. From pagan religious groups, to civil disobedience, to ecological sabotage (or ecotage), deep ecology is invoked as a philosophical, theoretical, normative, and intuitive foundation for belief, thought, and practice.

The term itself was first formulated, in 1973, by Arne Naess, a Norwegian philosopher particularly versed in Spinoza and Gandhi, and the originator of a radical type of empirical semantics (the Oslo Group). The original paper that explicated the conceptual and normative foundations of deep ecology (entitled "The Shallow and the Deep, Long-range Ecology Movements" and presented at the World Future Research Conference in Bucharest[38]) did not apparently attract a great deal of North American attention at the time. In fact it was close to a decade before deep ecology was to become a debated aspect of environmental theory.

In Naess's original article, he argued that the *shallow ecology* movement is characterized by a "fight against pollution and resource depletion." Its central objective was "the health and affluence of people in the developed countries." In distinction, the deep ecology perspective, he argued, presupposed

a. the "rejection of the man-in-environment image in favor of *the relational, total field image*"
b. *biospherical egalitarianism*—in principle. "The '*in principle*' clause is inserted because realistic praxis necessitates some killing, exploitation and suppression."[39]

The central distinction that Naess wanted to make by creating two streams within the environmental movement was as described above:

between a *reform* orientation and that of a radical perspective called deep ecology. This distinction is also meant as a highly charged means to demarcate the anthropocentric from the nonanthropocentric; the homocentric from the ecocentric;[40] the reductionist from the holistic.

Thus, deep ecology in its original formulation was essentially a critique of environmentalism based on what Naess viewed as the state-sanctioned (and thus coopted), short-term, economic, scientistic, resource-ist position of the emerging mainstream of environmental thought. Naess (as well as many of his North American followers) has gone to considerable lengths to make it clear that deep ecology is not to be understood as being opposed to reform environmentalism. Rather, it attempts to go beyond the instrumentalist reform orientation by posing "deeper" questions.

> The central issue is that of transcending ecology as a science, looking for wisdom through the study known as ecophilosophy, striving for an *ecosophy*—a total view inspired in part by the science of ecology and the activities of the deep ecology movement.[41]

On Naess's view, ecosophy is the vehicle through which the philosophical, and systematic expression of a new philosophy of ecological praxis can be articulated. In the words of Australian deep ecologist Warwick Fox, the basic intuition of ecosophy

> is the idea that we can make no firm ontological divide in the field of existence: that there is no bifurcation in reality between the human and the non-human realms . . . to the extent that we perceive boundaries, we fall short of deep ecological consciousness.[42]

Whether Naess would in fact agree that this was his basic intuition is unclear. It is clear, however, that Naess is interpreted as proposing that ecological consciousness is founded upon two ultimate norms: "self-realization" and "biocentric equality." These norms

> are not in themselves derivable from other principles or intuitions. They are arrived at by the deep questioning process and reveal the importance of moving to the philosophical or religious level of wisdom.[43]

Naess seems to have been very interested in the notion of questioning, and the relationship between the *deepness* of questioning and philosophy. Since the shallow or reform environmental movement lacks deepness of questioning, it generates different conclusions.

> In the shallow movement in favor of decreasing pollution and economy of resources, positions are tacitly assumed valid that are questioned in the deeper movement. But the differences in conclusions are largely due to certain questions, especially of value priorities, not being seriously discussed in the shallower movement. . . . The mainly technical recommendations of the shallow movement reflect the absence of philosophy rather than an unecological philosophy.[44]

Thus for Naess, beginning with an articulated set of ultimate norms, the deep questioning process will arrive at a deep ecological perspective. On this account then, for Naess the deep ecological perspective is defined via the *process* to reach it, not by the outcome of the questioning itself.

For Naess this openness to questioning without formalizing the domain of acceptable answers is what gives deep ecology its distinctive character. As Fox points out, should *un*ecological answers be defined through the deep questioning process, they would not be subject to recommendation because an unecological path would not satisfy the ultimate norms (self-realization and biocentric equality).[45] And as we shall see, for North American deep ecology, this provides access to a deep ecological position from a multitude of perspectives and traditions.

On a macro level there are two orientations to deep ecology. On the one hand there is Naess the philosopher, working on the philosophical and normative foundations of his own deep ecology, his own *ecosophy*. For Naess this project is (and ought to be) a highly idiosyncratic endeavor.[46] On the other hand, there is the North American deep ecology scene. For the latter, Naess functions as an authorial and inspirational signifier. But the immigration of Naess's ideas into the North American milieu has involved much more than translation from the Norwegian.

Over the years Naess has published very little in terms of extended outlines of deep ecology. His only book on the topic (published originally in Norwegian in 1976—*Okologi, samfunn, og, livsstil*) remained untranslated until 1989. Released in North America as *Ecology,*

Community and Lifestyle: Outline of an Ecosophy,[47] this work represents a considerable update and rewriting of the original in collaboration with American philosopher and environmentalist David Rothenberg. Written and structured in a rigid, formal fashion when compared to that of the typical warm and friendly prose of the North American deep ecologists, the direct popular influence of this book seems not to have been extensive.

In attempting to situate the writings of deep ecology (and writings of the radical environmental movement in general) the style of the prose — as a reflection of both the theoretical approach, and textual/literary antecedents is important. Since so much of deep ecological writing is tied up in evoking in the listener/reader pretheoretic intuitions about nature, the prose form comes to occupy important ground. This points to a critical failing on the part of North American deep ecologists. For Naess's part, he intentionally avoids imparting theoretical closure on deep ecology as he sees it.[48] He seems intent on creating a space in which the work of articulating deep ecology can take place; that is, deep ecology remains theoretically underdetermined precisely because, for Naess, the theoretical work has yet to be completed. The programmatic character and complicated style of Naess's work was taken less as a challenge to further develop and contextualize the philosophical system of deep ecology, than as an authorization to reify the concepts and construct a foundational program. In a sense, Naess's message seems to have been inverted. The challenge which Naess issued was to appropriate the *process* of ecosophical thought, a process that he performs with his work. Yet the absence of closure, and the emphasis on process seems to have been seen as an authorization for *anything goes.*

The adaptation of deep ecology into the milieu of North American environmental theory was accomplished predominantly via the work of George Sessions and William Devall.

In 1984 (during a camping trip to Death Valley), George Sessions and Arne Naess defined deep ecology's basic principles; these are typically referred to as the *deep ecology platform.*[49]

The platform is an eight-point normative manifesto that enunciates the ethical and political foundations of deep ecology. The platform hinges on an assertion about all things in the world possessing intrinsic value; this is the foundational move. Within the context of deep ecology this is the starting point for its ecological ethics. With the ethical foundation secured at the level of a totalized intrinsic value scheme, the platform develops a contextual picture of intrinsic value. Richness and diversity are taken to be the ecological expression of intrinsic value at work in the world. From here it follows that humans, in order to respect the moral standing of the world in its rich and diverse expression, must adopt a less intrusive and interventive role.

> Humans have no right to reduce [this] richness and diversity except to satisfy vital needs.[50]

This of course begs the question of the meaning of "vital," but leaving this aside we can see that this is the point where deep ecology creates a category map of humans as a unified group. The implication of this move to the outside reduces human agency into a single ethical goal: minimizing transgression of richness and diversity. Thus right from the beginning, there is a sense in which humans-in-nature become subjected to authoritarian constraints which issue forth from a normatively charged nature.

The political turn of the platform addresses population and ideology. Following from the intrinsic value of richness and diversity, the platform asserts that the flourishing of nonhuman life will require a significant reduction of human population, a change in the conception of life quality, and an alteration to "policies" to reflect these shifts.

Where and how such a substantial reduction of human population might take place is left largely undefined. In Naess's explanation the stabilization of population growth is presumed to take a great deal of time, and is implicit acknowledgment that profound alteration to global economic patterns is unlikely.[51] For Devall and Sessions, though, the point about population reduction is given added weight when they note that the world population is increasing at the rate of "one Bangladesh" per year.[52]

The overtly prescriptive content of the platform is itself interesting because Naess seems not to have been primarily concerned with ethics as such. Nor is he particularly concerned with grounding the rightness of behavior as the basis of moral action. Rather, Naess appears to be more interested in what sorts of *inclinations* naturally precede benevolent actions:

> Inspired by Kant one may speak of "beautiful" and of "moral" action. Moral actions are motivated by acceptance of a moral law, and manifest themselves clearly when acting

against inclination. A person acts beautifully when acting benevolently from inclination.[53]

Naess then would seem to be operating in a register that differs significantly from the tone and import of the "platform." Seeking expressions of "beautiful" action, Naess wants to determine the conditions upon which the inclination toward the beautiful might be fostered. This provocative idea is directed toward a sense of "environment" very much bound together with one's aesthetic presence within it. Naess situates his interests as located *prior* to ethics.

> I'm not much interested in ethics or morals. I'm interested in how we experience the world. . . . Ethics follows from how we experience the world. If you experience the world so and so then you don't kill. If you articulate your experience then it can become a philosophy or religion.[54]

As I will attempt to show, the North American version of deep ecology is a system of thought that seems to differ markedly from the aspirations and methods of Naess.[55]

Theoretical Fog

The development of this platform was the event that allowed deep ecology to claim a voice within the North American radical environmental movement. The proper interpretation of the platform has been a topic of considerable—and often heated—debate.[56] The articulation of a foundational philosophy to ground these points has spawned a great deal of interest from a number of disciplinary perspectives. Among the principle figures involved in this project have been Bill Devall, George Sessions, Warwick Fox, Alan Drengson, Delores LaChapelle, Michael Zimmerman, Gary Snyder, and John Seed. Together with this group there are a host of others writing from various perspectives on topics connected with deep ecology.[57]

The first North American, book-length elaboration and analysis of deep ecology was published by Devall and Sessions in 1985. I make use of this work not because it is deemed to be deep ecology's final word, its sacred text; although it clearly has been and remains an important text for the North American deep ecology movement.[58] Rather, I think it is useful precisely in the way that I have engaged the event of Earth Day. In other words, *Deep Ecology* presents itself in a more or less frictionless space. The successive reelaborations, the boarder wars, the internal disputes had not yet risen up around the newly organized concepts of deep ecology. In many respects much of what has been written on the topic since then is significantly engaged with responding to this work of Devall and Sessions.

The deep ecology of Devall and Sessions announces itself as "an invitation to thinking." Constructed about equally from text by the authors, and by a litany of quotes and excerpts spanning Lao Tsu to Gregory Bateson, it reads rather like a New-Age Bartlett's Quotations. The range of the official roll call that is evoked by Devall and Sessions is quite startling. An incomplete list includes: Gary Snyder, Theodore Rozak, Rilke, Dogen, Gandhi, Murray Bookchin, Pierre Clastres, Stanley Diamond, Carolyn Merchant, de Tocqueville, Morris Berman, Max Weber, Malthus, Blake, Spinoza, Heidegger, George Perkins Marsh, Paul Ehrlich, St. Francis of Assisi, Santayana, John Muir, Pascal, Robinson Jeffers, Aldo Leopold, Rachel Carson, Walt Whitman, Aldous Huxley, Goethe, Wordsworth, Colderidge, Shelley, Melville, Mark Twain, Mary Austin, D. W. Lawrence, Gilbert White, Fritjof Capra, David Brower, Fukouka, Li Po, Alan Watts, Whitehead, as well as a host of Buddhist, Christian, Taoist, and "primal" traditions.

In their introduction to deep ecological thinking, they describe deep ecology as

> a way of developing a new balance and harmony between individual, communities and all of nature. It can potentially satisfy our deepest yearnings: faith and trust in our most basic intuitions; courage to take direct action; joyous confidence to dance with the sensuous harmonies discovered through the spontaneous, playful intercourse with the rhythm of our bodies, the rhythms of flowing water, changes in the weather and the seasons, and the overall process of life on Earth.[59]

Deep ecology acknowledges that the policies and positions of "shallow" environmentalism are both necessary and useful, but involves itself with another more inclusive program to alter human consciousness. Developing a deep ecological consciousness involves work on the self, cultivating the sense that "everything is connected."[60]

Self, in the way that deep ecology invokes it, involves some kind of reading of Taoist traditions with respect to the organic self. As one of a multitude of appropriations, this conception of the self is explained by appeal to the Zen master Dogen:

> To Study the Way is to study the self.
> To study the self is to forget the self.
> To forget the self is to be enlightened
> by all things.
> To be enlightened by all
> things is to remove the
> barrier between one's self
> and others.[61]

The sense of self that interests deep ecology involves a complete break-down of the distinction between self and other; we recall Fox's *to the extent that we perceive boundaries we fall short of deep ecological consciousness*. This self that fades and dissolves into the world flows directly from the ultimate norm of self-realization.

> Spiritual growth, or unfolding, begins when we cease to understand or see ourselves as isolated and narrow competing egos.[62]

Thus the self that is to be discovered through the process of deep questioning is not really a self at all; there is an organic totality within which selves can participate through a deep ecological consciousness. It is only within this organic totality that the self/person can become whole (the many in the one). The basic position of deep ecology is that this process of becoming-whole, which constitutes the real work of deep ecology as personal praxis, amounts to a kind of metaphysical homecoming. It is not a process of creation, but of recollection. It is an invitation, as they say, to the dance, the dance of unity. Rather than appeal to a universal intuitive sense of recollection via a Jungian collective unconscious, archetype, and the like, deep ecology invokes a learning program that focuses on what is termed "the minority tradition":

> The type of community most compatible, in our estimation, with engaging in the "real work" of cultivating ecological consciousness is found in the minority tradition.[63]

The Minority Tradition

At first glance a concept of the minority, or the minor seems to hold a certain promise for thinking about social, and epistemological arrangements. Deleuze and Guattari, for example, write of the "minor" in relation to the uses of language. They speak of the "minor" and the "major" not as two different languages, but two different uses or functions of language.[64] The minor use of language consists in the ability to make language stutter from within. Deleuze and Guattari find exemplary expression of the minor use of language in Kafka, a Czechoslovakian Jew writing in German. But the minor is not solely involved with being foreign to a language:

> How many people today live in a language that is not their own? Or no longer, or not yet, even know their own and know poorly the major language they are forced to serve? This is the problem of immigrants and especially of their children, the problem of minorities, the problem of a minor literature, *but also the problem for all of us: how to tear a minor language away from its own language, allowing it to challenge the language and follow a sober revolutionary path. How to become a nomad and an immigrant and a gypsy in relation to one's own language?*[65]

The minor language is thus not a language constructed on the *outside* of language, it is an expressive language fashioned from within, from the major language itself. It is an ideolect that draws its creative potential from within the major. The minor, though, has a more complex set of meanings for Deleuze and Guattari; such meanings extend out from literature and language to encompass juridical and political references.[66] The majority always implies a constant, a standard by which evaluations are possible. From this point of view the majority always assumes the very attributes that are meant to distinguish it; the majority is not a numerical function.

> Majority *assumes* a state of power, not the other way around.
> It *assumes* the standard measure, not the other way around.[67]

The minority tradition, which writers such as Devall and Sessions seek to recover, is very much constituted by a sign reversal of the standard measures of the majority tradition that deep ecology identifies. Instead of being centralized, hierarchical, and oppressive, the minority tradition is decentralized, nonhierarchical, and democratic. They are also small-scale, governed by example, and noncompetitive. They are distinguished not by rapacious acquisitiveness but by a simplicity of wants. They are nonviolent and respectful of spiritual-religious mentors. They are ritual-based and tolerant of difference. And they have a more open communication with nature, and accordingly, a broader definition of community that includes the biotic.[68]

Deep ecology has interest in the minority tradition only insofar as it can be subject to deep ecological rendering; in other words, deep ecology is not attempting to theorize how "minor" traditions may maintain a subversive or revolutionary role in relation to a culturally dominant tradition. What I fail to see in this idea of minority is any sense in which it is internal to a majority. Rather, they seem to be positing a prior majority, and do so by inverting the dominant attributes of the present conception of majority.

In any case, their analysis of the operation of such a minority tradition brings them to a point at which they introduce anthropological explanation as the means to support a minor prior condition. Through anthropology they claim to derive evidence that

> authority need not be hierarchical and centralized. The "chief" was frequently noncoercive, primarily a ritual ruler and specific in dealing with members of the community.[69]

The appeal to the "primal" is a key move in deep ecological thought. It is part of the anterior-to-modernity construction, and it is part of the move to the outside that posits a preexisting humanness that precedes and underlies the artifices of modern life.

To marshal anthropological support for their characterization of the minor and primal, Sessions and Devall quote what they see as the "conclusion" of political anthropologist Pierre Clastres.

> One is confronted, then, by a vast constellation of societies in which the holders of what elsewhere would be called power are actually without power; where the political is determined by a domain beyond coercion and violence, beyond hierarchical subordination; where, in a word, no relation of command-obedience is in force.[70]

They take Clastres to mean that anthropology holds that there have been many societies where the political is without power.

Several things are of interest here. First of all, it is important to note that Devall and Sessions are not talking about a number of traditions (plural) that all have similar characteristics; they are talking about a single tradition with the characteristics outlined above. It is found, they say, in many other cultures and historical eras. This includes Native American traditions, Eastern traditions, the Paris Commune of 1871, Spanish anarchists in the 1930s, Thomas Jefferson, Walt Whitman, Woodie Guthrie (IWW?), Carl Sandburg, Ursula LeGuin, and others. This is, they say, a persistent tradition. The invocation of Clastres is meant to extend their suspicion into a prehistory of human nature.

To be clear about this, Clastres in no way makes the "conclusion" upon which Devall and Sessions mount their expansive claims about the minor. The passage quoted above is part of a rhetorical paragraph that falls midway through a critique of the developmental ethnographic model that assumes, among other things, that political power is only manifest in relationships that are essentially coercive. What Clastres attempts in the larger context of the quoted passage is to lay bare the traditional ethnographic position from which the problematic of power is typically posed. Clastres makes a fairly straightforward argument about the ethnocentric foundation of ethnology, and the not-so-secret kinship between ethnology and Western ideology.

That Sessions and Devall appeal to this passage as "evidence" for the ubiquitous character of the minor tradition would tend to compromise the force of the minority program.

Aside from an apparent misreading of Clastres, *Deep Ecology* falls into the same trap that Clastres is attempting to escape: the ideological position that sees the "primitive" as an embryonic, not fully formed version of ourselves; the propensity to see the political and economic organization of "archaic" cultures as somehow more pure because, lacking certain features of "civilized" society, their life must be more decentralized, nonhierarchical, democratic, and so forth. That primitive cultures (on deep ecology's account) are not spoiled by the pernicious aspects of the modern, creates a figure of the primitive that is charged symbolically with redemptive possibilities. Essentially this is a story of another Fall; modern humans, having transgressed natural and ecological connections with the earth have been cast out of the Garden;

primitive humans, having remained resistant to this mode of development now retain a proprietary relationship with authentic, ecological living. I will return to Clastres and this thematic of the primitive.

To summarize, I have been discussing how deep ecology has been constructed in North America, how it relates to environmentalism in general, and how the move to the outside grounds and structures the deep ecological vision. But before we can give more consideration to how humans come to occupy the deep ecological world, how the minority tradition translates and maps onto a story about what humans are and ought to be, we need to step back and look in broader terms at how environmentalism—in general—is related to its historical and cultural context. In the next chapter I will address, from several different points of view, the construction of environmentalism (and environmentalism as a construction) in relation to ecology, system, and totality. To accomplish this, we will, so to speak, come off the mountain—the place where the move to the outside becomes visible—and attempt to engage environmentalism on the level of its relationships to other theoretical concerns.

2

Ecology/System/Totality

Prosthetic Ecology

Perhaps the most that can be said of environmentalism as it exists today in the West (in light of the above specified topology of positions and exceptions internal to the field itself) is that it has something to do with Western perceptions of its relationship with, and obligations to nature; something to do with an interpretation of ecology; adherence to some notion of a *systems view*;[1] and some sense of the present state of nature as being in a condition of crisis. In short, environmentalism stands as a conflicting set of representational systems.

What has emerged as environmentalism is not a monolith of agreement or complicity, but a number of modes of practice, thought and theory that embark from some point of a counter-reading of the way we treat the world. The crisis that seems to be agreed upon is the threat of the breakdown of critical natural systems that sustain life on the planet. Belief in the crisis, and more importantly, the diagnosis of the crisis condition and the construction of its etiology provide both the shared content of environmentalism, and the locus for the emergence of conflicting interpretations. On the one hand, the recognition of crisis has motivated the construction of an environmentalism that attempts to reform existing practices in order to avert ecological disaster. This would be deep ecology's *Other*: shallow, or reform environmentalism. On the other hand, the crisis is read differently. Specifically, the crisis is seen as an indication of a more fundamental problematic that cannot be solved via superficial reforms. In other words, whereas the existence

47

of ecological threat is agreed upon, representations of it are not. The rather tenuous connection between these polar ends of environmentalism is Ecology.

It is important to make clear at the outset that ecology has several important connotations. Scientific ecology is very much a branch of population biology. Its primary concern is the relationship(s) between biotic and abiotic systems. In biological discourses, terms such as diversity, stability, resilience, ecosystem, stress, and so forth, have a very precise and descriptive meaning. And even if the utility of these terms is contested, such disputes are essentially matters of an empirical sort; that is, disputes may in principle be settled by appeal to the degree of *fit* between a theory and the actual relationships it is purported to describe. On the other hand, what we might call popular ecology is more of an explicitly normative adoption of some of the language and concepts of scientific ecology. Whereas for the scientific ecologist, a term like diversity is used to predict, for example, niche size or energy throughput, the same term in its popular usage becomes much more concretely a value.[2] This question of the relations between ecology and science is important. Ecology, in addition to offering what is taken to be an alternative image of things, is in most respects virtually consonant with the dominant scientific modes of reason. The concepts upon which it relies—system (open/closed), ecosystem, feedback, stability, resilience, diversity, niche, succession, competition, cooperation, and so on—are often as mechanical, economic, Cartesian, and instrumental as traditional modes of scientific thought.

There is a near universal assumption within environmentalism that scientific ecology provides both a real model of how the world actually is, and a prescriptive model of how we as humans ought to fit in. Of course by *fit in* it may mean that we don't fit in at all, but the point is that ecological theory, by being placed as if in an homeomorphic relationship with the "real," both describes a state of affairs, and prescribes and (therefore) legitimates various political, ideological, and moral positions with respect to the world.

As a theoretical apparatus, scientific ecology introduces no new epistemological rupture into the fabric of Western thought. To the extent that claims to the contrary are made on behalf of ecology, we need to take a closer look at the social and political context in which these claims are made; for it is here that one can begin to see the way ecology operates conceptually in a prosthetic arrangement with environmentalism. As a prosthesis, ecology gives to environmentalism a very potent set of metaphors with which to talk about the world.

Ecology-as-prosthesis functions on the one hand as a device that develops normative articulations about the world, and on the other hand obscures the very normativity of its articulations through ecology's claim on the objectivity of science. In this sense it is a very powerful prosthesis indeed; part of its achievement is to obscure its artificial character.

For many environmental writers, ecology is understood as marking a kind of objective finality of science itself; the final truth about the world is made manifest in and through ecological theory. But this lofty aspiration for the universal truth of ecology comes about in the same manner and via the same procedures that the post-Enlightenment scientific project has itself come to be constructed in the universal.

> The phantasm of science is double: on the one hand there is an "epistemological break" that relegates all other thought to a senseless prehistory of knowledge and, simultaneously, on the other hand, there is a linear accumulation of knowledge, hence of truth as a final totalization.[3]

The description offered here by Jean Baudrillard is, I think, useful. What he is pointing to is how—in general—the rationalist eschatology of science sheds light upon the theoretical position which ecology attempts. By seeking to be a new theory of everything, ecology claims not only a *relatively* advanced position (because as a theory it temporally succeeds other theories), but an *absolutely* more advanced position, because by taking itself as a universal theory, as an end, it can account for its own prehistory.

This we could call the paratheoretic movement of ecological theory. Paratheory in this context is a maneuver that turns resistance to a theory into an instance of verification *for* that theory. Hans Blumenberg describes paratheoretical constructions thus:

> Internally, it protects one from doubts, and externally it destroys the resistance, by categorizing assent to the theory as a symptom of rationality and inner freedom, indeed as an ethical accomplishment, and putting the reasons for the resistance to it beyond the pale, as extratheoretical and scientifically and morally indefensible.[4]

We could certainly ask whether or not the double movement, the "phantasm" of science that Baudrillard describes marks a kind of totalization of paratheory. In other words, we could ask whether science, on this account, would be intrinsically paratheoretical. To do so would draw us toward more general considerations of scientific legitimation. But we needn't attempt to sort through this problem here. We need only reach an agreement that any epistemological break which ecology claims is only visible from the foundational site of science itself; and thus we are presented with a question-begging circularity.

From the point of view of environmentalism, ecology-as-prosthesis thus provides a rhetorically potent device. A device that, on the one hand, has the ability to claim the authority of sameness with science; this would be the claim to legitimation. On the other hand, it simultaneously asserts its difference from science; a difference that founds and supports its "ethical accomplishment." To the extent that ecology acts as a descriptive and prescriptive template for environmentalism, we need to ask what the nature of this relationship is. To begin with, what difficulties are presented by the fact that the environmental position is to some extent modeled within the same discursive constellation (i.e., technoscientific) as the culture it attempts to problematize. As I will discuss below, this problem tends to collapse into more fundamental questions.

A good deal of energy is taken up amongst environmentalists attempting to set limits and meanings on the terms and concepts of ecology; yet little effort has been expended looking at the way ecology functions as an enabling or legitimating discourse (i.e., what interests and impulses does ecology serve? what does ecological discourse authorize and what does it exclude?).

In scanning the intellectual and theoretical history of ecology (and the domains to which its contemporary versions are heir), one is confronted with a multitude of ideological, spiritual, theological, transcendental, and mystical inscriptions. In our consideration of environmentalism and ecology, we need to begin to probe some of these inscriptions, and attempt to outline the semiotic character of the prostheses. This is not to suggest that the relationships can be reduced to the movement of signs. To make such a claim would be to maroon oneself from the irreducibly material character of ecological threat. There are more than signs at stake. The semiotic question simply allows one to point out that the instant in which nature becomes, for instance, an "ecosystem," a transformation takes place such that nature is no longer *merely* the natural world. It becomes a sign, which—apart from any claim to scientific specificity—connotes as well certain social and moral obligations. With this in mind, we need to ask whether the critique of environmentalism that focuses too narrowly on ecology as science becomes unwittingly engaged in a kind of straw man project.

State Ecology

Ecology (or *Oekologie*), from the Greek *oikos*, meaning household or living place, was first described by Ernst Haeckel (1834–1919) in 1866. Ecology was defined as the branch of biology that was to deal with the relationships between organisms and their living place, or environments. The sense in which *oikos* was used was closely tied to the Aristotealian sense of the word where the state of the household could be thought of as the condition of the State. Haeckel's development of the idea of ecology is thought by some authors to have begun with a much clearer political than scientific posture. In her book *Ecology in the 20th Century: A History*, Anna Bramwell sets out the complexities of Haeckel's monism, his anti-anthropocentrism, and his belief in an ordered, and progressive nature.[5] She describes him thus:

> Haeckel's link with ecology is not confined to the verbal accident of inventing the term. Ecology, as a conceptual tool, was a term that contained the kernel of its normative usage from the beginning. Its founder became heavily involved in politics. Both his politics and scientific work touched on concerns fundamental to today's ecologists. . . . Haeckel's most important legacy was his worship of Nature, the belief that man and nature were one, and that to damage one was to damage the other. He offered scientific 'proof' that harmony and benevolence were intrinsic to the world, and that man must fit into its framework, while cherishing and caring for nature's wonders.[6]

Haeckel's observations were largely founded on work done by plant geographers in the nineteenth century. Alexander von Humboldt, for example, devoted his life to the correlation of the various world vegetation types with the prevailing climates. This work in plant geography was founded (at least in part) on the eighteenth-century concept of the economy of nature; essentially the idea that the apparent disorder observable in the natural world was grounded in a basic constancy or harmony. It was a way of reconciling disorder and waste in nature (e.g., plant seeds that never reach maturity) with a belief in a rational God in control of His creation. Through the economy of nature it was possible to see the world as a dynamic balance between all living things. It was during this time that concepts such as food chains, predation rates, and species range began to take shape.

The idea of an economy of nature fell from grace, as it were, when the evidence for the occurrence of "extinction" was generally accepted in the nineteenth century. From this point on, the concepts of struggle and competition largely replaced the harmony assumed by the economy of nature.[7]

Ecology as science, as an account of the world, and as the assumed master text for environmentalism, has had a spectacular effect on conceptualizations of the way in which the natural world (including human societies) function and relate. This is not to say, however, that ecology has simply transformed historically from Haeckel's normative monism to a scientific holism. Consider, for example, the claim that ecology, together with the systems view, posits the world as a network of interrelated systems; a fairly standard and uncontroversial claim, but one that can be supported in radically different manners.

> Ecology . . . is the study of systems at a level in which individuals or whole organisms may be considered elements of interaction, either among themselves, or within a loosely organized environmental matrix. Systems at this level are named ecosystems, and ecology, of course, is the biology of ecosystems.[8]

This was written in the late 1960s by the Spanish ecologist Ramón Margalef. He attempts to launch a cybernetic revolution within ecology in order to account for the complexities of the natural world. Margalef sought to shift the problematic of ecology from physiology and behavior to a more abstract region where it was possible to speak of the ecosystem as a "channel which projects information into the future."[9]

As a counterpoint to Margalef, consider the following, written by one of the preeminent American ecologists, Eugene Odum:

Ecology is the study of households, including the plants, animals, microbes, and people that live together as inter-dependent beings on Spaceship Earth . . . the environmental house within which we place our human-made structures and operate our machines provides most of our vital biological necessities; hence we can think of ecology as the study of the earth's life-support systems.[10]

Here the claim of interdependence is supported by appeal to the house-hold, the *oikos*. Houses within houses, the human suburbia within the spaceship metropolis, Odum's account is clearly framed within more popular ecological conceptions. Yet it seems to me that both of these accounts—one systematic and abstract, the other anthropocentric and instrumental—conceal a theoretical kinship that consists in the unifica-tion of the world-as-system. Two very different sorts of reduction are involved: from world to channel, and from nature to the ideal of the well-managed house. But at the root, what binds these two visions of ecology together, is a move to the outside that renders the earth a con-tainer, and simultaneously, everything on it becomes *contents*. The link, of course, is the malleable concept of "system."

Ecology and System

To the extent that ecology operates as the conceptual framework through which we may come to perceive the world-as-system, and given that ecological systems can be thought of in vastly disparate fashions, one is struck by the degree to which this ambiguity remains unchallenged.

One way to account for at least some of the polyvalent character of the notion of *system* and the so-called *systems view* (insofar as envi-ronmentalism is concerned), would be to understand it as a wishful extension of work done in 1940s and 1950s by the Austrian biologist Ludwig von Bertalanffy (1901–72). Bertalanffy's work was synthesized into a large-scale project that came to be know as General Systems Theory (GST).

A biologist by training, Bertalanffy attempted to launch a revolt against what he saw as the great paradox of the modern scientific pro-ject. The accomplishment of science he felt to consist in its having clearly demonstrated a world of enormous complexity. Physics, chemistry, microbiology, all of these domains had theoretically advanced at such a pace in the last century that the problem of complexity itself was coming to be a unified scientific concern. Yet at the same time as the world becomes revealed scientifically as a problem in complexity, Bertalanffy claimed that reigning scientific models were incapable of accounting for this complexity. Modern science, he felt, had brought us to the brink of understanding something profound about the world, but because of the very poverty of its own methods, it could take us no further. In this sense complexity was a kind of remainder generated by the reductive algebra of the scientific method. Bertalanffy's vision was to revolutionize the algebra in such a way as to internalize the remainder.

At a basic level Bertalanffy's systems view is an attempt at a reorientation of the scientific perspective. Systems, properly understood, would allow an understanding of the world that contemporary science could not accomplish on its own. To think on the level of systems is to take as the object of investigation not a conglomeration of parts, but a dynamically interacting *whole*. It is not an attempt to say an understanding of parts is no longer relevant; rather, it is that the kind of thinking that is required to understand parts is qualitatively different from the kind of thinking that can account for larger slices of reality. Bertalanffy framed the problem as follows:

> The system problem is essentially the problem of the limitations of analytic procedures in science. This used to be expressed by half-metaphysical statements such as emergent evolution, or "the whole is more than the sum of the parts," but has a clear operational meaning. "Analytic procedure" means that an entity investigated be resolved into, and hence can be constituted or reconstituted from, the parts put together, these procedures being understood in their material and conceptual sense.[11]

The application of the analytic procedure or tradition is characterized by Bertalanffy as involving two critical moves: that the interaction between parts be bracketed off from consideration; and, that the relations describing the parts be linear such that equations describing the parts be of the same form as equations describing the whole.[12] Thus the partial processes implicit in the parts are simply summed together to construct an *additive* image of a totality.

Bertalanffy's dream was apparently to create a unified theory of all systems.

[T]here exist models, principles, and laws that apply to generalized systems or their subclasses, irrespective of their particular kind, the nature of their component elements, and the relation of the "forces" between them. It seems legitimate to ask for a theory, not of systems of a more or less special kind, but of universal principles which are valid for "systems" in general.[13]

This optimistic program was grounded in the search for isomorphic relations that could allow unifying claims to be made between—as far as traditional disciplines were concerned—disparate phenomena. The central conceptual tool that founded the systems view—and is also axiomatic to scientific and popular ecology—is the idea of *open* and *closed* systems.[14] The Newtonian universe is a classic example of a closed system;[15] given knowledge of initial conditions (position, gravity, velocity, etc.) at a specified point it is then possible to predict the state of a given body at any subsequent point in time. Bertalanffy's system view challenged the scope and applicability of the teleological, closed system model.

The open system, on the other hand, is always operating in a specific *context*. It cannot be isolated from its environment, precisely because it is in constant interaction with it.[16] Bertalanffy's reconceptualization of the world as an interconnected series of open systems had a clearly normative program at its foundation:

The unifying principle is that we find organization at all levels. The mechanistic world view, taking the play of physical particles as the ultimate reality, found its expression in a civilization that glorifies physical technology that has led to the catastrophes of our time. Possibly the model of the world as a great organization can help to reinforce the sense of reverence for the living which we have lost in the sanguinary decades of human history.[17]

A systems view very similar to that advocated by Bertalanffy has become infused into contemporary ecological thinking. It is interesting to note that other versions of systems theory have been less influential to ecological thought. For example, the works and concepts of other theorists such as Ervin Laszlo (cognitive maps), Eric Jantsch (self-realization),

Arthur Koestler (the holon), or Gregory Bateson (recursion and difference), provide a set of rich philosophical tableaus that could considerably extend and enhance ecological thinking.[18] Yet it is principally the organicist thinking that inspired Bertalanffy and others[19] that is most evident within contemporary ecological and environmental discourses.

Translation

A particularly striking example of early expressions of systems thinking and ecology can be found in Barry Commoner's *The Closing Circle*.[20] Commoner's project was to list the "laws" of ecology in a nontechnical language.

Everything is connected to everything else;
Everything must go somewhere;
Nature knows best; and
There is no such thing as a free lunch.

This fairly straightforward group of maxims was taken by many environmentalists as a high-powered critique of Western society. Each of these pop-ecology slogans conceals and advances system-theoretic principles.

Everything is connected to everything else speaks to concepts of relationship and interdependence, and the property of wholeness.

Everything must go somewhere refers to the idea that in the contextual setting of systems, there is no *out there*.

Nature knows best (perhaps a reformulation of Goethe's "*Nature is always right*"?) advances the realm of nature as something that is both independent of human intention, and self-evidently correct.

And finally, *There is no such thing as a free lunch* (perhaps one of the best one-line critiques of late-capitalism) is directed at the notion that there is always an *effect* associated with alteration to a system. As Tony Wilden put it, causes cause causes to cause causes.

The new setting in which these laws of ecology found their juridical home became the fuzzy concept of the ecosystem. The term "ecosystem" was apparently coined by Sir Arthur Tansley in 1935. The ecosystem, Tansley wrote,

is the idea of progress towards equilibrium, which is never, perhaps, completely attained, but to which approximation is made whenever the factors at work are constant and stable for a long enough period of time.[21]

The ecosystem as an organizing principle allows one to think about the behavior of organized groups of organisms. It foregrounds an idea of stability and equilibrium. Ecosystem as concept has proved to be a powerful tool. In addition to fostering a relational and contextual understanding of the natural world, it brings an organicist conception of nature, via science, into popular discourse about the environment. In very potent terms, it draws nature (and often society) into a metaphorical and medical image of a body. The body of the earth as organism, the earth as (sick) patient—two figurations that mark a Copernican turn in environmental thinking. The move to the *outside* presumed necessary in order to grasp the earth *qua* organism, accomplishes this efficient medicalization. Such planetary figurations of the earth make for irresistible recourse to other medical and biological representations (the death of lakes, rainforests as lungs, wetlands as kidneys, ozone as epidermis, the Third World as genetic sperm bank). The Earth and its Organs. And as Wilden points out vis-à-vis Bateson and Lévi-Strauss, the same system analogies can construct of "culture" the organic "mind" that is missing from the body analogy of nature.[22]

The idea of ecosystem, both on Bertalanffy's account of systems and Tansley's description of ecosystem proper, was not assumed to be a realm independent of humans, a realm outside of culture. The gradual exclusion (most often implicit) of humans from most accounts of the ecosystem is something that has taken place in the last forty years. In most popular and scientific writing the ecosystem is a place that does not include a human presence; and if it does, that presence is most often a very specific kind of human: specifically, the figure of the "primitive," which in turn is usually organized into a privileged ecological space— "wilderness." Part of what we might call the moral force of the ecosystem concept attaches to the fact that the ecosystem is something that enculturated humans are constantly excluded from (and thus always poised to transgress).

Ecological Patois

Articulations of scientific ecology such as Commoner's laws of ecology were and are important for a number of reasons. First of all, as a biologist, Commoner's work marks perhaps one of the most significant and influential attempts to translate scientific ecological discourse into mainstream environmentalism.[23] In the same manner as *Jurassic Park* packaged chaos theory into a parable of *nature will find a way*, ecological theory was thus rendered into palatable sound-bites. In the process of translation, two things happen: ecological principles become softened to a point where there is no particular fixity to their interpretation; and nature becomes defined as an independent otherness to which humans are both subjected, and removed. In the first instance, ecology is asserted to be basic and understandable. Its principles and axioms according to Commoner are clear enough to be understood by all. In the second, nature as a totality becomes an infallible arbiter of earthly affairs—*nature knows best*, or to once again resurrect Hardin, *nature will commensurate the incommensurables*. And the earth, as the embodiment of this totality of nature, becomes a system closed and indifferent to the epiphenomena of modern culture. Commoner would argue that his position is not that the earth is a closed system precisely because it receives energy inputs from the sun. My point is that his axioms describe a material closure within the economy of earth-based ecosystems. In other words, he invokes a one-way thermodynamic necessity.

The work of Commoner exemplifies the opening-out of scientific ecological discourse into the field of environmentalism. The insights of ecology as science became recast as axioms for environmentalism. Yet these axioms are stripped of the discursive specificity of the scientific domain in which they were formulated, and have become free-floating normative concepts with the stamp of scientific approval. Put differently, the environmentalization of ecology may be understood as the production of ecological signifiers. These signifiers, however, do not partake of any determinant relationships with signifieds. The movement of signification only finds completion within a collective practice of discourse.

Neil Evernden has argued that what "ecology" has done for environmentalism amounts to providing a socially legitimate way of speaking about *pre*theoretic intuitions about nature. For Evernden, in *The*

Natural Alien, there is always an unmediated experience of nature that grounds the environmental impulse. However, he points out, using ecology in this fashion extracts a high price. The qualitative, pretheoretic intuitions experienced by the (idealized) environmentalist are progressively replaced by a quantitative theoretical detachment which Evernden claims ecology provides. So, in the rush to gain a socially legitimate voice the environmentalist has embraced a discourse that turns his/her "passionate involvement" with/in nature into that of a "dispassionate observer."[24]

By adopting the language and insights of ecology, Evernden argues, the environmentalist

> has had virtually to forsake his *raison d'être*. In learning to use numbers to talk about the world he forgets that his initial revolt was partly precipitated by people using numbers to talk about the world.[25]

But Evernden makes an important mistake here, and his mistake hinges on precisely the kind of discursive elasticity that environmentalism—and ecology—demonstrate. Evernden supposes that the environmentalist in the state of nature—that is, the environmentalist who is unsullied by the "mechanistic assumptions" of scientific ecology—will feel moved to speak out against the destruction of nature in a protest that is "essentially a protest on behalf of value."[26] And further, that far from being the "subversive science" that Rozak described in 1972,[27] ecology actually undermines the *true* environmental position.

Evernden wants to argue that the environmentalist in his/her haste to speak out for nature seized upon ecology precisely because it offered the promise of a nonsubjective voice, a voice that while not truly reflecting his/her motivations, offered nonetheless a language within which to speak of nature. The price extracted, concludes Evernden, is that in doing so she will surely lose sight of the real reason for being an environmentalist to begin with. Environmentalism, Evernden tells us, has been a failure. A failure because of a discursive and epistemological contamination (scientific ecology as virus). Whereas I tend to agree that Evernden reached the correct conclusion about the failure of environmentalism, I think he is correct for all the wrong reasons.

If there is an evil genie, a Faustian bargain, it is not to be discovered in ecology. Simply put, the *ecological patois* that the environmentalist speaks is filtered to such an extent that it bears little resemblance to theoretical scientific ecology. By focusing on a particular conception of ecology *qua* science, and a particular conception of the objectivity of science, I think that Evernden loses sight of the way ecology actually gets deployed. The upshot is that our attention gets focused within an argument about a kind of ecology that is simply not part of common usage within environmentalism.

Translators of ecological theory—such as Commoner, or Capra, or Lovelock, or the deep ecologists I have referred to—are not involved in mapping *pure* scientific principles onto environmental discourses any more than Bertalanffy was involved with purely objective (read, traditional) science. In all of these cases there is an explicit attempt to inject a normative and ethical foundation. And there is a sense in which the science under translation becomes framed as a new and total science; where the scientific *is* becomes the moral *ought*, and where objective detachment and dispassionate observation become the site of ethical responsibility and subjective involvement.

My point here is not to argue that ecology is of no interest to a critique of environmentalism; simply that since ecology is not a stable category, it must therefore be considered in the specificity of its use (i.e., context). Ecology is a remarkable device for producing signs about the world, but it is necessary to realize that the "ecological view" is as far from a purely scientific position as it is from an epistemologically consolidated one. If ecology as such has no fixed meaning with respect to environmentalism (and this is at least in part why ecology as a foundational discourse can be used to such radically different ends), then the important questions have to do with what the affinities are between the impulses or intuitions of environmentalism, and the insights and intuitions of ecology.

Some theorists will take the position that regardless of the intent, there is a strategic aspect in the adoption of ecology. Striking an allegiance with a "scientific" discourse can be thought of as an effective tactic for deploying science as a Trojan Horse containing dissenting ideas. For example, Murray Bookchin writes:

> The explosive implications of an ecological approach arise not only because ecology is intrinsically a critical science— critical on a scale that most radical systems of political economy have failed to attain—but also because it is an integrative and reconstructive science. This integrative, reconstructive aspect of ecology, carried through to all its implications, leads

directly into anarchic areas of social thought. For, in the final analysis, it is impossible to achieve a harmonization of man and nature without creating a human community that lives in lasting balance with its environment.[28]

I doubt that Bookchin would still agree with his ecological idealism, but the idea that ecology is somehow essentially subversive, a science unlike all other science, has found a comfortable niche within the contemporary environmental *geist*.

There are, however, other theorists such as anarchist writer George Bradford that see ecological science as a tool that is useful to the extent that we understand its limits and applicability.

> Ecology as science speculates, often with profound insight, about nature's movement and the impact of human activities on it. But it is ambiguous, or silent, about the social context that generates those activities and how it might change. In and of itself, ecology offers no social critique, so where critique flows directly from ecological discourse, subsuming the complexities of the social into a picture of undifferentiated humanity as a species, it goes astray.[29]

Bradford's point here is profound. It is unfortunate that he represents such a marginal voice within the greater environmental community. A more common interpretation, different from both Bookchin and Bradford, is that ecology simply *is* what ecology *does*. Donald Worster, for example, concludes that the idea of ecology has constantly been a shifting ground. Thus, he says, there is a choice to be made as to how ecology will be harnessed in the contemporary world. Moreover, he suggests that the natural and historical affinity of ecology with moral values will create an ecological or scientific ground for ethics.

> Ecological biology, while in general reinforcing certain values more than others, has been and remains intertwined with many of man's ethical principles, social aims, and transcendental ambitions. There is no reason for believing that this science cannot find an appropriate theoretical framework for the ethic of interdependence.[30]

But I think that the important question here is not whether the adoption of ecology has, so to speak, backfired; the specific character of

ecology is always contingent upon external, and preexisting requirements. Rather, it appears that ecology presented itself as a strategic way
of structuring the world that in and of itself could be made compatible
with any number of environmental intuitions.

Modernity

I want to suggest that ecology has been harnessed to fulfill an impulse
(or perhaps compulsion) that lies as much at the heart of environmentalism and deep ecology as it does at the heart of modernity. This function of ecology in relation to environmentalism marks what we could
call a *will to totality*; an intense desire to construct a total account.
Aware as I am that the whole question of modernity and postmodernity
constitutes an embattled intellectual and cultural zone, a few words on
what I mean are in order.

A useful attempt at a very broad definition of modernity would be
to assert that it is neither entirely a sociological concept, nor political,
nor historical. Rather, it is a characteristic mode of civilization,

> which opposes itself to tradition, that is to say, to all other
> anterior or traditional cultures: confronting the geographic
> and symbolic diversity of the latter, modernity imposes itself
> throughout the world as a homogeneous unity, irradiating
> from the Occident. . . . It acts as an ideational force and prin-
> ciple ideology, sublimating the contradictions of history in
> the effects of civilization. . . . Thus as an idea in which a
> whole civilization recognizes itself, modernity assumes a reg-
> ulatory cultural function and thereby surreptitiously rejoins
> tradition.[31]

While not, perhaps, the final word on the subject, I find this appealing
because it situates modernity as a *mode* of being aware of one's location—culturally, historically, sociologically. It is self-legitimating solely
on the grounds "that it is more up to date, newer, and thus more valid
in relation to a vision of history as progress."[32]

To broaden this out somewhat, and to delimit modernity less in
terms of force, and more in terms of the self-certainty of the modern
subject, Mark Taylor describes the philosophical project of modernity:

In the wake of Descartes's meditations, modern philosophy becomes a *philosophy of the subject*. As the locus of certainty and truth, subjectivity is the first principle from which everything arises and to which everything must be returned. With the movement from Descartes, through the Enlightenment to idealism and romanticism, attributes traditionally predicated of the divine subject are gradually displaced onto the human subject. Through a dialectical reversal, the creator God dies and is resurrected in the creative subject. As God created the world through the Logos, so man creates a "world" through conscious and unconscious projection.[33]

The will to totality that I refer to here, is to construct an account that subsumes both past and present conditions into a rational unfolding of history. The kinship between this desire and that of modernity is that both are founded upon the historic emergence of science as a way of positioning the rational observer, and both specify a rational and knowing subject. Ecology as an organizing force is very much an artifact of modernity in the way that Baudrillard constructs it. Ecology is foremost a homogenizing force that flows from the Occident. It thus assumes the regulatory force that Baudrillard characterizes as intrinsic to the function of modernity. What Taylor demonstrates is the operative position, and the transparent self-consciousness of the *knower* within modernity.

The ecology question in environmentalism turns out to be a displacement; the discursive elasticity of the discourses of ecology renders it a malleable and ambiguous zone of radical environmentalism. The critique of radical environmentalism must therefore go beyond the question of ecology and ask more fundamental questions. The sorts of questions I have asked in this chapter have led to an impasse; we see that radical environmentalism is marked by a desire to undertake certain kinds of organizational practices with respect to the world. The tools and conceptual frameworks that are deployed in the service of this desire are clearly of less concern here than that desire in itself.

For the purposes of this discussion, I will divide the question of the desire for totality into two separate but related ideas. The first has to do with the relationship between radical environmentalism and Enlightenment, and how radical environmentalism occupies an untheorized and potentially dangerous position in this regard. The second aspect of the will to totality will be discussed in relation to the way that radical environmentalism represents modernity as an historical process.

Enlightenment

The relationship between myth and enlightenment that is described in Horkheimer and Adorno's *Dialectic of Enlightenment* is particularly pertinent to our critical discussion of radical environmentalism[34]; primarily from the point of view of foregrounding the confused relationship between Enlightenment ideals and deep ecology.

The *Dialectic of Enlightenment* concerns itself with the domination of nature as a result of a self-destructive aspect of the Enlightenment. Enlightenment itself, on Horkheimer and Adorno's account, is inextricably bound up with domination.

> Myth turns into enlightenment, and nature into mere objects. Men pay for the increase of their power with alienation from that over which they exercise their power. Enlightenment behaves towards things as a dictator towards men. He knows them insofar as he can manipulate them. In this way their potentiality is turned into his own ends. In the metamorphosis the nature of things, as a substratum of domination, is revealed as always the same. This identity constitutes the unity of nature.[35]

An objectified nature, a space of objects and resources, is what makes domination both possible and inevitable. Their hypothesis is that Enlightenment modes of rationality function in a way similar to that of myth in pre-Enlightenment cultures.

> Man imagines himself free from fear when there is no longer anything unknown. That determines the course of demythologization, of enlightenment, which compounds the animate with the inanimate just as myth compounds the inanimate with the animate. Enlightenment is mythic fear turned radical.[36]

The fear of the *outside* that is stabilized by the function of myth, is covertly repeated through Enlightenment practices of quantification and abstraction. The outside, that which cannot be otherwise represented (or tolerated), no longer exists. Positivism stands as emblematic of this "universal taboo" against the outside.[37] This persistent point emerges repeatedly throughout this work. The first encounter with it was as the move to the outside. We then saw it in another form as the foundation of the systems view and deep ecology. And here we can make a theoretical shift that allows this observation to be put into correspondence with Enlightenment.

> To the Enlightenment, that which does not reduce to numbers, and ultimately to the one, becomes illusion; modern positivism writes it off as literature.[38]

But enlightenment for Horkheimer and Adorno, in addition to exemplifying a particular mode of instrumentality (i.e., rationality), is also the basis for freedom. Thus the object of a critical theory, or a negative dialectics is not in the overthrow of enlightenment as such, but in the subversion of the uncritical assumption of progress vis-à-vis enlightenment. The paradox of enlightenment is that the same process that creates human autonomy and freedom creates alienation, repression, and a profound loss of freedom. The process of disentanglement from the hold of enlightenment was a critical, not a mythological project. To the extent that we witness in radical environmentalism a retreat from enlightenment writ large, the cause of this, say Horkheimer and Adorno, is not to be found within the nationalist, pagan, primitive Nazi, and New Age mythologies that mark such a retreat, but from within the Enlightenment itself.

> Just as the Enlightenment expresses that actual movement of civil society as a whole in the aspect of its idea as embodied in individuals and institutions, so truth is not merely the rational consciousness but equally the form that consciousness assumes in actual life. The dutiful child of modern civilization is possessed by a fear of departing from the facts which, in the very act of perception, the dominant conventions of science, commerce, and politics—cliché-like—have already molded. . . . The same conventions define the notion of linguistic and conceptual clarity which the art, literature and philosophy of the present have to satisfy. Since that notion declares any negative treatment of the facts or of the dominant forms of thought to be obscurantist formalism or—preferably—alien, and therefore taboo, it condemns the spirit to increasing darkness.[39]

Thus there is a totalized effect which is characteristic of enlightenment that thwarts attempts to articulate differences.

It is characteristic of the sickness that even the best-intentioned reformer who uses an impoverished and debased language to recommend renewal, by his adoption of the insidious mode of categorization and the bad philosophy it conceals, strengthens the very power of the established order he is trying to break.[40]

The *Dialectic of Enlightenment* speaks in many ways to concerns that are shared with environmentalism, but does so in a way that presupposes a critical awareness on the part of environmentalism that is simply not there. In many ways, environmentalism has adopted the position of "the best-intentioned reformer"; underwriting change through the very concepts and categories spawned by the ostensive object of change, environmentalism unwittingly assists in the cunning of enlightenment.

Deep ecology attempts to reenchant the world, to rediscover the place and function of myth and magic, and it attempts to do so through its representations of the "minority tradition." Within the this tradition deep ecology seeks to recover a nondominating science, a successor science[41] that is based on a way of knowing wrought and practiced through myth and ritual; ecology is given this role. Though at this point, one is again reminded of Horkheimer and Adorno: mythic reasoning is a mode where

everything unknown is alien and primary and undifferentiated: that which transcends the confines of experience; whatever in things is more than their previously known reality. . . . The dualization of nature as appearance and sequence, effort and power, which first makes possible both myth and science, originates in human fear, the expression of which becomes explanation. . . . [T]he separation of the animate and the inanimate, the occupation of certain places by demons and deities, first arises from this pre-animism, which contains the first lines of the separation of subject and object.[42]

While this might be an overly functionalist account of the role of myth and ritual, it nonetheless puts into question the privileged role which deep ecology ascribes to them.

To the extent that myth anticipates enlightenment, Horkheimer and Adorno want to push this further to say that enlightenment itself as it progresses becomes "more deeply engulfed in mythology."[43] As Tim Luke points out, one does not have to look much further than texts like Capra's *Tao of Physics* to find a certain resonance with this idea.

> Enlightenment science cannot be disinvented or destroyed. It is fully embedded in many of our existing acts and artifacts. Sensuous, participative, metaphysical views of reality—when fused into technical potentials of modern science for destructive misapplication—could promote a more domineering rather than a less destructive science. There are no guarantees.[44]

What we are faced with, and what most needs to be developed in this argument about the confusing fog of deep ecology, is to expose the conflation of enchantment and instrumental rationality. On a number of levels, this odd mix of the modern, antimodern, antirational, and future-primitive is similar to the ideological climate that developed around the *völkisch* movement in turn-of-the-century Germany; this too was a time of reaction to modernity and industrialization, progress and alienation.

> Repelled by the egotistical, commercial and spiritless mentality of modern economic society, *völkisch* writers called for renewed contact with natural and cosmic forces which, while inaccessible to the rational mind, were capable of rejuvenating and transforming the increasingly mechanized German spirit. According to *völkisch* ideologies, these cosmic forces were at work in the common language, traditions, art, music, social customs, religion, blood, and soil which united a particular *Volk*.[45]

Paul Monaco, in *Modern European Culture and Consciousness*, defines the *völkisch* ideological climate of pre-war Germany as a "reactionary consciousness." In contrast to revolutionary consciousness ("the harnessing of the rebelliousness in humans to specific ends determined by the course of history and by materialist necessity"), reactionary consciousness

> is, by contrast, de-evolutionary. It draws upon the past, but it does not trace a continuum down the centuries toward a desired state of present being. Rather, it evokes the lost characteristics of human experience, which are collective, ritualistic, and primal.[46]

The relationship to the present, to the modern, is always constrained by a longing for an imagined past. This, together with an essentially organicist notion of culture, community, and nature allows the reactionary consciousness to develop always in terms of a *lack* in relation to the perceived forces of the modern. This form of consciousness is

> a state of awareness that is in rebellion against the loss of community, the loss of identity, and the loss of a sense of transcendence. Reactionary consciousness rebels against loneliness and anomie, against rationalism and materialism, against the artifices of human progress and technology. In seeking to ameliorate the condition of spiritual and emotional impoverishment brought on by modern life in industrial societies, reactionary consciousness marks an atavistic flight from nearly any aspect of experience that may be called modern. In the flight, the pursuit of a return to nature, or the embrace of instinct over reason, or the quest to recognize links between people which are racial rather than historical, are common.[47]

In his analysis of the condition of German ideology in the Weimar Republic, Jeffery Herf attempts to explore the paradoxical character of modernity in Germany; that is, the selective pursuit of modern technology together with a rejection of Enlightenment reason.[48] His thesis is that National Socialism involved an unlikely melding between the pre- or antimodern and the modern.

> Nazi ideology was a reconciliation between the antimodernist, romantic and irrationalist ideas present in German nationalism and the most obvious manifestation of means-ends rationality, that is, modern technology.[49]

By attempting to draw some theoretical momentum from a critique of Enlightenment science and technology, radical environmentalism opts only to question the *content* of the story, not the foundational impulse itself. This environmentalism says only that Enlightenment conceptions of nature and humanness were *wrong*; it does not consider the operations that create and impose the fixed and eternal categories of nature and humans, nor does it challenge the validity of such categories.

It is not my intention to make an extended argument about the similitude between *völkisch* ideology, reactionary modernism, and radical environmentalism. Aware as I am of the rhetorical force, and the heavy-handedness of implying a link between the *blut and boden* ideology of National Socialism and deep ecology, to remain silent about the resemblance of the salient characteristics would defy the whole point of critical inquiry. To the extent that deep ecological theory does become engaged in more than a perfunctory critique of the Enlightenment or modernity, it tends—in a mode reminiscent of Herf's and Monaco's outline of Germany—to advocate a position that it constructs as anterior to modernism. Habermas topologically situates this pre- or antimodern impulse as "old conservative" in relation to cultural modernism. A position which "in view of the problematic of ecology, allows itself to call for a cosmological ethic."[50] We see this perhaps most clearly in the privileging of the idealized figure of the "primitive." The critique of the modern, of technology and progress, ends up advocating a poorly defined *retro*-ecological ethic.

Through the operation of identifying a deficiency in modern conceptions of rationality *qua* instrumentality, technology *qua* alienation and domination, and science *qua* objectivity and reduction, there is a widespread tendency to vilify these ideals themselves, and not the characteristic mode(s) in which they have been realized throughout the various developmental settings of modernity. Clearly there are linkages and similitudes in the ways that modernity has developed throughout the world. There are, however, differences that are equally important. If the "modernity" of Horkheimer and Adorno was made too similar to the concept of Enlightenment itself, it is perhaps that they viewed Enlightenment in total through the lens of the experience of Germany. As Herf points out, viewing modernity "through the prism of Auschwitz . . . they mistakenly attributed to Enlightenment what was in fact the product of Germany's particular misery."[51] The deep ecologists are perhaps subject to a similar tunnel vision that sees modernity only through the prism of North American traditions of modernity. This allows them to rebel against what they identify as the pervasive forces of the modern writ large, without clearly articulating either an adequate theory of modernity, or a position exterior to it (whatever this might be).

Modernity as Paradigm

Reason, science, technology, history—such things are simply not critically assessed in terms of their place and function within the total narrative structure of modernity. One is pressed to think of one example in the literature where modernity is analyzed in terms of its totalized, foundational, and universal narratives. Far more common is a tendency to think of modernity as something like an operational set of beliefs and practices, something like a "paradigm" in the sense that Kuhn described the concept.

For example, Max Oelschlaeger writes:

> Clearly the movement is edging toward a new and comprehensive vision of the relation between humankind and the natural world. . . . Paradigmatic revolution is in the wind . . . and humankind may be on the brink of a postmodern age.[52]

So viewed, radical environmentalism is a radical response to the paradigmatic condition of modernity. Modernity-as-paradigm seems simply like a set of rules which we (like Kuhn's "normal scientist"[53]) follow until the anomalies reach some sort of critical mass. Modernity is taken to be an historical epoch, characterized by certain instrumentally useful technologies and beliefs. By sensing paradigmatic revolution in the wind, Oelschlaeger is suggesting both the need, and the opportunity to "shift" paradigms. Modernity is thus characterized as having reached its end, and no longer able to generate new ideas within its paradigmatic construction, previously—within modernity—unthinkable paradigms now become possible candidates for a postmodern age. His vision of *post*-modernity can mean only *after modernity*, and its structure is an empty vessel waiting to be customized to suit our deep ecological needs.[54]

The trope of the "paradigm" accomplishes an astonishing transformation to the meaning of modernity for Oelschlaeger. Clearly, by paradigm Oelschlaeger is not drawing directly on Kuhn's sense of the term; all that Kuhn ended up wanting to do with the term (in the fifteen years following the publication of *The Structure of Scientific Revolutions*) was preserve it in order to speak of shared commitment within scientific communities. The term entered his original research because

> I . . . could not, when examining the membership of scientific community, retrieve enough shared rules to account for the group's unproblematic conduct of research. Shared examples of successful practice could, I next concluded, provide what the group lacked in rules. Those examples were its paradigms, and as such were essential to its continued research. Unfortu-

nately, having gotten that far, I allowed the term's application to expand, embracing all shared group commitments. Inevitably, the result was confusion.[55]

So how then are we to interpret the way in which the concept of "paradigm" functions as an organizing principle for modernity? If not by Kuhn's sense, then presumably it can be taken in a more colloquial sense to mean "worldview," or paradigm in some far more general sense; for example, after George Grant: "The principle of any paradigm in any civilization is always the relation between any aspiration of human thought and the effective conditions for its validation."[56] In any case, by first allowing modernity and postmodernity to be descriptively organized as paradigms, then implicitly framing the concept of paradigm as the determined result of active human will and aspiration, it becomes possible for radical environmentalists to claim defeat over the theoretical force of modernity/postmodernity; just as we may will ourselves out of modernity, so may we will the condition of the postmodern.

The deep ecologist Alan Drengson, has written extensively on this idea of "paradigm shift." His book *Shifting Paradigms: From Technocrat to Planetary Person* develops a deep ecological, neo-Kuhnian paradigm model.[57] However, his interpretation of Kuhn selectively focuses on historical continuity *between* paradigms. By remaining outside of the debates engendered around the question of *intra*-paradigm commensurability,[58] Drengson circumvents any serious consideration of relativism. With historical continuity assured, Drengson can call for an epistemological and cognitive revolution without having to cope with the problem of incommensurability.[59] Although Drengson is not working specifically with(in) a construction of modernity, he nonetheless characterizes the contemporary ecological scene as ripe for new (old) mythologies.

Oelschlaeger, Drengson and other radical environmental writers see the contemporary crisis (for Oelschlaeger, in modernity, and Drengson, in ecological viability) as an opportunity to formulate replacement cosmologies, to speak new and ecological metanarratives. Oelschlaeger calls for "a new creation story or mythology," in the hope of leading humankind out of "the homocentric prison into the cosmic wilderness." The criteria for the new paradigm for the "postmodern age": "it must have both scientific plausibility and religious distinctiveness."[60]

In the absence of serious consideration of the complex attributes of the Enlightenment heritage, radical environmentalism can only reproduce its effects through the construction of new total accounts. Regardless where we situate ourselves vis-à-vis modernity/postmodernity (i.e., modernity is over, modernity is in its last phase, modernity is incomplete, etc.), it is mistaken (and perhaps dangerous) to view it as a paradigm. Precisely what is at stake in the postmodern debate is the *possibility* of a paradigmatic condition; the theoretical suspicion is in fact that the rules for constructing paradigms have been rendered radically suspect. The critique of modernity must be well enough informed to observe that the edifice of Enlightenment thought is collapsing under the weight of precisely that tendency toward universalized, paradigmatic constructions. To establish a "position," such as this idiosyncratic notion of the postmodern, that is beyond the modern, that somehow transcends the historical horizon of metaphysics, is to extend the reach of the modern into new regions of universality.

In relation to the movements of ecology, system, and totality, the paradigmatic tendency that I have been describing points to a fundamental trap into which this environmentalism has fallen. One formulation of this trap would be to say that it has reacted to the totalizing strength of the modern by means of an equally strong and totalizing alternative. At the very moment when the claims of Enlightenment rationality are revealed as a pretense of omnipotence, the response is one of equal strength. At the very moment when the dreams of Science and Progress and Truth are disclosed as the parlor games of the modern, as the ground of Western metaphysics, the response is a dream of *overcoming*, of being somehow outside. It is a substitution, as Vattimo has said, of "a new truth for an old error."[61] It is as though modernity was something that could "be put aside like an opinion."[62] It is as though the disclosure of the limits of *les grands récits* of the modern has been taken as an invitation to put in place a new *grand récit*. As Lyotard put it in his *Libidinal Economy*:

> we do not want to fall into the trap set by this rationality at the same moment that it is vanquished. This trap consists quite simply in *responding to the demand of the vanquished theory*, and the demand is: put something in my place. The important thing is this place, however, not the contents of the theory. It is the place of theory that must be vanquished.[63]

And the demand is, *put something in my place*. If environmental thought is to extract itself from a reactionary mode, if it seeks a position where it may indeed have something "new" to say, must it not attend to the larger forces and flows which found and constrain critical and radical thought?

To summarize, in this chapter I have been looking at how deep ecology is situated simultaneously within and against modernity and Enlightenment. I have looked at how it operates in the service of a will to totality: (re)making the world as a system. And I have argued that the question concerning ecology as such is really a displacement; the question concerning ecology and environmentalism is really a question about the relationship(s) between environmentalism, modernity and Enlightenment. The move to construct the world as a system is paralleled by a move to simultaneously mystify nature in such a way that humans come to occupy a position of *natural* opposition to nature. And nature becomes a solitary and undifferentiated totality of laws.[64] The peculiar relationship that deep ecology apparently has with modernity is rendered historically significant by observing that a similar rejection of the modern and a return to nature was also of great importance to the *völkisch* political movement. I argued that deep ecology manifests a similar condition of reactionary modernism that preceded the rise of National Socialism. The very selective critique of modernity that is undertaken in deep ecological literature manifests itself in a wish to construct a futuristic premodernism. The "postmodern age" is thus taken to be an opportunity to reconstruct a presumed prior organic unity. In the next chapter, the third and final component of this critical engagement of deep ecology, I will shift perspective and look in more concrete terms at the consequences for humans as a result of this return to nature. In particular, I will look at deep ecological accounts of the human subject, the way deep ecology is organized around a problematic argument about anthropocentrism, and how the figures of both the "primitive," and "wilderness" operate as ecological smoke-screens for what amounts to ecological colonialism.

3

Displacing the Humans

There is no master narrative that can reconcile the
tragic and comic plots of global cultural history.
—James Clifford, *The Predicament of Culture*

Back to the Pleistocene!
—Earth First! slogan

Nature Knows Best

In this chapter, I will argue that in the total picture of nature as eluci-dated by environmentalisms like deep ecology, modern humans occupy a position on the outside. This is accomplished through a dou-ble operation that begins with a move to the outside, and simultane-ously, the establishment of a foundation for holding modern humans apart from nature. This search for a ground zero, for a total account, is as repetitive a moment in the development of the discourses of environ-mentalism as it is in the development of post-Enlightenment thought. What we witness in the past two decades are attempts to move to the outside, to develop and reify larger and more encompassing metaphors. Robust ecological metaphors provide a picture of complexity in which any (human) intervention implies a risk.

In modern terms the most total ecological metaphor is the organi-cist metaphor (which for our purposes has passed from Ludwig von Bertalanffy's grand synthesis, through Ashby and Weiner and Margalef, to Commoner, Shephard, and Lovelock). As discussed above, organicist slogans such as *the whole is more than the sum of the parts*, have been common currency in the environmental movement for years. The use of

75

such slogans is taken to be a kind of incantation to proclaim a new and ecological understanding of things. *The world isn't like a machine, it's like an organism.* But what kind of organism? Accounts vary. Sometimes it is like a cybernetic organism (whatever this turns out to mean), sometimes it is like a very large single organism, or superorganism (Lovelock), and sometimes the organism metaphor means that all significant processes can be reduced to, or understood as, biological.

The problematic aspect of the organicist metaphor is in the total reduction of the human to the biological. This often takes place as a masking of the culture/nature opposition, whereby nature becomes the totality of laws into which humans are entirely absorbed. (We recall Commoner: *Nature knows best.*)

The kind of holism implied by *the whole is more than the sum of the parts* can easily obscure the fact that the parts are still granted an ontological primacy over relations. Moreover, it can also obscure the value of wholes in creating social and historical characteristics of parts in their contexts or environments.[1] Through a kind of ideological mirror game, organicist metaphors flatten out relations on the inside. What exactly are the relations that are being subsumed into the totality of nature? To start with, they are the increasingly ubiquitous global social relations of (post)industrial capitalism. Following this, we could point to other relations of social hierarchy, domination, and oppression—from women to "minorities"—that are overwritten through organicist projections.

The status (political, economic, social, historical) of marginalized groups, and more importantly, attempts by these groups to assert and theorize difference in the face of their historical status as Other(s) is jeopardized again and finally through this organicist move: the ultimate melding of ideology and essentialism—*we* are all one. The contested categories, women, native, minority, the poor, nonwhite, Third World are no longer sites of discursive and political negotiation; the legitimation of difference is threatened directly through what amounts to the imposition of a totalized piece of bio-ideo-colonialism. An imposition that undermines attempts to politicize or radicalize the category "difference."

There is a strange set of operations that take place here. First of all there is an identification of some fundamental problematic with respect to the relationship between culture and nature. Economically, this is typically framed as having to do with *nature* being historically used as an instrumentally valuable set of resources, and *culture* seeking only to maximize wealth by selectively commodifying natural resources. But this picture of nature as external, mute, and instrumentally valuable, is only part of the culture/nature problem for environmental thought.

Through a process of reversing signs and valencies of beliefs, the modern conception of *nature as other*, is progressively replaced by the conception of *culture as other*. The ecological self, the self we would apparently encounter on the path not taken by contemporary Western society, becomes more than an authentic conduit to nature, it *becomes* nature. For the ecological self, this change in identification allows for more direct involvement and empathy with the natural world; *I am the mountain, I am the rainforest*, and so forth. But the nonecological self and the mass of contemporary society exists in a fallen state; we are a kind of polluted nature, a nature polluted by modern culture.

On this account, the perfect ecological space must be one that is absent of *modern* humans; for such humans are polluted. In the *natural* order of things, the order currently authorized (primarily) by the science of ecology, humans, and the culture by which they have been infected, have come to occupy a position as a kind of pollution. Mary Douglas talked about the shifting notion of dirt or pollution as "matter out of place,"[2] but in radical environmentalism, culture becomes matter out of place, and humans approach the status of *placeless matter*.

On Evernden's account, humans are exactly that—exotics:

> The phenomenon of the exotic organism is one that seems indicative of a systemic "misunderstanding": the organism seems unable to make sense of its place in the community it finds itself in. . . . [T]here are grounds for regarding humans as exotics of a sort, since technological innovation may effectively cast its creator out of context. But it may be that the source of human indeterminism and ambiguity is more fundamental than that of an environmental misfit. Perhaps the very mode of development of our species is such as to inhibit the refinement of the perceptual abilities which could facilitate our occupancy of a particular place in the organic world.[3]

Evernden advances an essentially deterministic *misfit* argument. (Although the argument for humans as misfits is equally an argument for humans as special; which repeats—in a way that Evernden perhaps missed—the Cartesian separation of humans from the rest of the world.) In any case, the determinism in Evernden's argument is propelled through both technology and biology. Through technology, Evernden supposes that humans have transgressed a natural connection with nature, removing us from some fundamental and prior *being* in nature. But the more inflexible argument is that humans, through some kind of evolutionary decision have adopted a forever-young phylogenetic strategy. Evernden develops this idea of evolutionary youthfulness through appeal to the biological notion of neotony—the retention of juvenile characteristics by adult descendants (i.e., paedomorphosis). On Evernden's account, humans inhabit a perpetually juvenile evolutionary state; a state in which an organism is

> indeterminate in its being and unrelated to its environment. It is an undecided, uncommitted creature awaiting resolution.[4]

Humans, it seems, must *await* resolution, a kind of scientific rebirthing; as if under the sign of a biological reality principle, fulfillment of the human project is always deferred until some later date. Humans become other in relation to nature, waiting in an alienated, immature state to find themselves, to come home again. Where human agency was once bound up in a world of resources and objects with potential or realized utility, we now face an ecological world where human agency itself is conceived to be a transgression of a natural (read, humanless) order.

The general position of radical environmentalism seems on the surface to involve the framing of problems such that nature's status as Other is problematized; the very idea that nature is a realm external to humankind is brought into question. We are directed implicitly or otherwise to a critique of a dualism presumed to have had its historical locus in the writings of Descartes. The direction of this argument is nearly always *from* nature *to* humans; we are part of nature, and not the reverse. The epistemological result of this maneuver is that nature becomes subjectified and humans are subsumed into the organic and inorganic totality of a subjectified nature as specified by ecology. Difference (that is taken to be a given on the Cartesian account—subject/object, self/other), comes to be discernable only in terms of relative levels of organization.

The meaning of this bracketing-off of difference to the politically and socially marginalized is clear: questions of power, hierarchy and subjugation within and between human groups are less important than the relations of humans *in toto* to nature. The subjectifying of nature, and hence the undermining of attempts to understand difference, marks a novel (though perhaps not all that new) kind of colonialism; a colonialism that this time operates ostensibly in the name of nature.

Voices attempting to gain access to a legitimate (read, non-subjugated) subject position (i.e., a subject position that is not transcendent, universal, centered, and "rational"), are once again overwritten. The subject can no longer be an autonomous, rational, centered subject, because this is the tradition that has built a nature-hostile worldview of subjects and objects. Nor can there be a radicalized conception of subject as operating and resisting in and through particular cultural and social contexts; this would offer no guarantee that nature would be granted a privileged status. All that remains is an ecological subject that is an inclusive, participating component *of* nature, that speaks only of, and through nature. Culture, history, difference and resistance become externalities in the production of an ecological present; the human subject goes under erasure in this process of immigration into ecological space.

This environmental position marks a new kind of foundationalism. This is a foundationalism that naturalizes the world as "ecological," and as we have seen, legitimates this process through an imagined grounding in science. This foundationalism allows environmental theory to be constructed such that it accounts for contemporary ecological threats by imagining an idealized past; a past that marks both beginning (origin), and a utopic projection of an end. The two figures that bear much of the weight of this foundational program are that of wilderness, and "primitive" humans; these two figures will be dealt with in more detail below.

The Anthropocentric Circle

The argument about anthropocentrism figures into this problem with environmental thought. Anthropocentrism is given a great deal of theoretical force in radical environmental theory. It is used in *ad hominem* fashion to label *shallow* environmentalism, and it is used in general to mark any mode of thinking that foregrounds and privileges human value.

The intervention/tautology that all human views are and must be *human* views (and therefore necessarily anthropocentric) has been discussed by Warwick Fox. Fox points out two different senses of the term anthropocentrism. The first is the tautological sense in which things thought by humans are inescapably human thoughts; the second sense has to do with the unwarranted differential treatment of nonhuman beings on the basis of the fact that they are not human. Conflation of these two senses Fox dubs the *anthropocentric fallacy*.

> Whenever the anthropocentric fallacy occurs in ecophilosophical discussion, or whenever moves are made in that direction, it should be pointed out immediately that while all human views are equally anthropocentric in the trivial sense of the term ("all our views are human views"), they are stunningly different in the significant (chauvinistic, imperialist) sense of the term, that is, in the extent in which they set humans as all-important or at least morally superior to other beings and, hence, in the extent to which they advocate or at least legitimate the relentless exploitation of the nonhuman world by humans.[5]

As a first-order diagnostic or categorizing tool, anthropocentrism cleaves environmentalism based upon its normative position regarding nature. To be *non*-anthropocentric is to be granted membership into the radical wing of environmentalism. The non-anthropocentric environmental position seeks not human requirements above all else, but attempts, in some sense, to speak for the world (that cannot speak for itself).

We can see that what the anthropocentric distinction does—in relation to dominant (Western) historical conceptions of the relationship between humans and nature, self and other—is to set up a reactionary position; a position which we might call the anthropocentric circle. By railing against the world-hostile representations of Western late-capitalist practice(s), radical environmentalism cautions us to be mindful of the toxifying results of maintaining on the one hand the polarity of ethically endowed subjects (read, humans), and on the other, morally neutral objects. The nonanthropocentric position then, is one that challenges the representational practice that frames the nonhuman world as objects and resources.[6] This position asks that we stand up and protest in the name of the world that cannot speak for itself. *Think like a mountain*, speak on behalf of the whales, or the aboriginals. And this is the point where the anthropocentric argument comes full circle. Speaking on behalf of nature (whether this means mountains or whales, or "others") is still a representational operation that requires an authorized agent, and an object in need of representation. The only difference between environmental and other representational practices, is that environmental representations attempt to *cloak* the human role as representer. Instead of being a "scientist," the radical environmentalist seeks the position of ventriloquist.[7] This wish to provide a voice for the world, to engage in a kind of ecological orientalism, is a hallmark of deep ecological theory.[8]

American deep ecologist Bill Devall is skilled at ventriloquism:

> When humans investigate and see through their layers of anthropocentric self-cherishing, a most profound change in consciousness begins to take place. People stop identifying exclusively with their humanness and begin a process of transformation of their relationships with other beings . . . 'I am protecting the rainforest' develops to 'I am part of the rainforest protecting myself. I am that part of the rainforest most recently emerged into thinking.'[9]

The rainforest, in this case, is re-represented through the words of a deep ecologist: *I am the rainforest.* That there may be actual indigenous humans living in the rainforest that the deep ecologist wishes to become is not a problem: the proclamation of the ecological self would be: "*I am* a forest being."[10]

What then is the political import of the anthropocentric circle? This is a complex question; perhaps a better one would be to ask what's wrong with saying "I am a forest being?" In this latter we can see the representational practice I have been talking about, but we can also see on another level a displacement of human agency such that difference (human/forest, deep ecologist/aboriginal) is recast as sameness. Again we see that the human subject has a tendency to vanish into a nature organized by radical environmentalism.[11]

Through its analysis of contemporary practice, and by erasure of the independent, modern human subject, the *becoming-mountain* position brings all humans into the topography of ecological space. On this account the ecocentric position is easily aligned with an *eco*-affirmative, misanthropic agenda. Non-ecocentric humans as a cancerous invasion into the body of nature, ecocentric humans as self-appointed antibodies.[12]

By framing all things human into the binary opposition ecocentric/everyone else, we are implicitly asked to assume the heterogeneity of the category "human." By engaging an unproblematized notion of humans as a group, the anthropocentrism argument bypasses consideration of the contextual nature of human agency. What this argument ends up saying is that the environmental crisis is more about humans *qua* category, than it is about, for example, the global structure of production and consumption, or capitalist class structure, or patriarchy, or orientalist constructions of others, and so on. From the point of view of (economically, politically, and historically) marginalized and subjugated groups, an apparent attempt to circumvent an analysis of power, hierarchical and coercive social practices, in short, the move to the outside, can easily become an attempt to blame the victim(s).

To return briefly to our discussion about Enlightenment and modernity, and the proclivity for the radical environmental agenda to situate itself in a position anterior to modernity, several additional points and some summary observations can be made. To begin with, once contemporary humans are defined as Other in relation to nature, culture becomes defined as *naturally* intrusive and beyond the realm of nature proper. The culture/nature distinction, so forcefully established and maintained through Enlightenment philosophy, becomes reified from the opposite perspective. Following this line of thought, rationality, science, progress, and technology, the prime schemas grounding the development of Western culture, are deemed to be part of the *modern*, and thus part of the problem. The reaction, though, is not to question the operations, but to wish them away by constructing a story about an ecologically harmonious premodernism (or a posthistoric primitivism).[13] There is a growing anti-Enlightenment mood within the radical environmental movement, and in general within Western New Age communities of thought. A resurgence of interest in primal traditions, earth-centered religions, the mystical, and the spiritual over the rational, and a renewed focus on the personal over the political, are all symptomatic of this anti-Enlightenment trend.

Wilderness and the Mirror of the Primitive

"Wilderness" has a deceptive concreteness at first glance. The difficulty is that while the word is a noun it acts as an adjective.

—Roderick Nash,
Wilderness and the American Mind

So begins Roderick Nash's classic work on American wilderness. Wilderness has not become any less deceptive in the nearly thirty years since Nash first published *Wilderness and the American Mind*. What is this place called wilderness? Indeed, is it a "place" at all? For deep ecology, the ontological character of wilderness seems to be as a space devoid of culture, devoid of civilization. Metaphysically, wilderness stands as the realm of the real, the well-spring of life, and as mirror in which is reflected *authentic* experience of the world.

The idea of wilderness has enjoyed a continuous vogue in North American nature writing from the time of Henry David Thoreau. Contemporary debates concerning wilderness take place on a number of levels. From an economic point of view, wilderness has become an operative concept to define the preservation, conservation and management of scarcity—both of physical spaces, and of the genetic *capital* contained within those spaces. From a political point of view, wilderness marks a contested zone of ownership and use. And from the radical environmental point of view, wilderness is the place where nature resides. The context of the primitive existence, as we describe and construct it, *is* wilderness.

Wilderness is a perfect space utterly absent of (modern) human presence. Wilderness marks, in a way similar to that of the primitive, an operation that defines through a kind of *via negativa* what we are, through stating what and where we are not, and cannot be. This is an operation which redoubles the culture/nature opposition by seeming to switch the privileged term of the opposition. This modern wilderness has passed from a conception of moral wilderness, both a place and an idea of evil and darkness (think of Hawthorne's *The Scarlet Letter*), a place that was identified with the (soulless) red man, to become simply an absence and an apology. It is an empty space through which is acknowledged the transgression of human presence. Wilderness in this picture is Other. It is presumed to present a surplus of meaning in relation to dominant modes of expression. In other words, wilderness as signified exceeds its signifier. And perhaps this would go some distance to account for why wilderness is so often mystified; its contents are presumed to be far larger than its form. This is the figure of the secret of wilderness: a Nature with contents too big for its form. It contains secrets larger than itself.[14] It is in this sense that the "significant" part of wilderness is its own remainder; that part of itself which exceeds its own signification. This manner of wilderness does not include humans, and in a certain sense which I shall attempt to show, wilderness does not include primitives either.

One recent attempt to update and explore the field of wilderness thought and studies, is the book by Max Oelschlaeger, *The Idea of Wilderness: From Prehistory to the Age of Ecology*. I have already looked to this work to demonstrate the problematic characterization of modernity/postmodernity that is undertaken in radical environmentalism. We need now to look more carefully in general at the thematic of wilderness and its associative term, the primitive, in light of the theoretical arguments developed thus far. It will be interesting to look more closely at the stakes that are involved in an operation that makes of humans "just plain ecological citizens." And I will attempt to dismantle the wilderness/primitive configuration in such a way that we can ask what a *post*environmental position might look like. The implicit question here is what kind(s) of subjectivity can we hope for in our imaginings of possible futures. Is it possible (or desirable) to for(a)ge a path, as future primitives into the ecological space of wilderness? Or is this desire a mask for the well-worn spirit of imperialism which seeks to specify a future based on its fabrication of a past?

Oelschlaeger argues that a conception of wilderness has been fundamental to the very nature of human existence since times prehistoric. In *The Idea of Wilderness*, Oelschlaeger attempts to do for wilderness what Clarence Glacken did for historical conceptions of nature in *Traces on the Rhodian Shore*, and what Roderick Nash has done for wilderness in the history of America.[15] The difference between Oelschlaeger's work and that of Nash and Glacken is that in the former, the work is situated well beyond the bounds of a traditional historical investigation.

From its conception and construction of the primitive, to the essentializing of gender, through its critique of modernity and idiosyncratic understanding of the notion of the postmodern, to its apotheosis of the American wilderness writers Thoreau, Muir, Leopold, Robertson Jeffers, and Gary Snyder, Oelschlaeger's book is an attempt to articulate a totalized and universal history of wilderness. More importantly, the book is presented as an antidote to the abyss between contemporary theory and environmental thought. It is presented as a radical historical record of the idea of wilderness. It seeks to recover the Paleolithic idea of wilderness, and what he assumes to be the harmonious, ritual-based social/natural customs that exemplified Paleolithic—that is, primitive—culture(s).[16]

One could be inclined upon reading this work to treat it as a philosophical attempt to understand wilderness in light of a particular reading of ethnographic and historical records. But this kind of reading, it seems to me, opens only a space in which to engage a *philosophical* position on the basis of what is written. But as an attempt at ecological/philosophical theory, this book needs to be engaged differently; as theory it has to be taken as the product of certain social and historical conditions, and needs to be subjected to a social and political analysis—not simply a philosophical one. Thus rather than treating this work as a piece of philosophy, I choose to frame it as a work of ethnography. As such we can begin to ask different sorts of questions; questions which focus on Western practices of self-fashioning. For the critique of ethnography is the critique of ethnographic authority; the authority to represent, the authority to speak for others, the authority to construct others.

Primitive Others

"In Wildness lies the preservation of the world."[17] These words of Thoreau transform into the wild*er*ness mantra that grounds *The Idea of Wilderness*. The "er" is a hinge which mediates between a quality or intensity of wildness, the unruliness and strangeness of being wild, and the piety of an idea or place of an empty wilderness. It seems to me that wildness is always held in abeyance in the deep ecological wilderness; as though wildness constitutes the repressed of this modern wilderness.

First and foremost, this modern wilderness is salvific. The project is to rediscover *our* primal origins, and in doing so to recover this salvific principle. But it is more than a principle or ideal; wilderness for Oelschlaeger both mediates the relationship between humans and nature (i.e., wilderness as an epistemological boundary zone, a zone where we negotiate ourselves in relation to nature), and, simultaneously, wilderness is literally a place as well (i.e., wilderness as a physical location where one would be in the presence of real nature). The goal of his project is to construct some idea of a "posthistoric primitivism"—the meaning of which I will attempt to develop.

The idea of wilderness is traced through four phases or moments: "Paleolithic (prehistoric), ancient, modern and postmodern." Accordingly, he modestly admits, his study assumes the stature of "the natural history of humankind" (p. 4).[18]

The privileged moment, and the point at which an origin is identified, is the Paleolithic. Posthistoric primitivism is thus an attempt to reinvest contemporary culture with an originary sense of wilderness, where the human consciousness does not make (impose) any firm ontological distinction between its enterprise and the natural world. In short, posthistoric primitivism attempts to realize Fox's point that *to the extent that we perceive boundaries, we fall short of deep ecological consciousness.*

We begin with a fairly uncontroversial claim: cultures existed prior to Sumeria and Egypt; and the manner of individual existence was not entirely Hobbesian—nasty, harsh, brutish, and short. Yet in order to make his claim seem controversial, and even radical, Oelschlaeger repeatedly constructs a counterposition, variously termed *the modern mind, the modernist, the modernist view*, with which he imagines a heated debate. Undaunted by his observation that "as inquiry turns to the deep, deeper, and deepest past, it seems to exceed the bounds of legitimate research" (p. 7), he proceeds to construct a Paleolithic ethnography. We are presented with the same two figures—wilderness and the primitive—that provide a normative and ontological structure in general for deep ecology; only in this instance, rather than discontinuous artifacts and antecedents being crafted into a whole, we have total, continuous history in the making.

If we can only unhinge ourselves from "the lens of history," he tells us, we can begin to see into the Paleolithic mind. To this end, Oelschlaeger outlines and argues several claims that collectively characterize the primitive.

Oelschlaeger surmises that the Paleolithic hunter-foragers likely believed that irrespective of place, nature was home.[19] This is an important claim for Oelschlaeger and deep ecology because it allows the argument to be made that the original idea of wilderness was no idea at all:

> The idea of being lost in the wilderness logically necessitates a geographical referent conceptualized as home as distinct from all other places. . . . They could not become lost in the wilderness, since it did not exist. (p. 14)

There was no *out there* for the primitive, they were themselves coterminous with the natural community.

In such a world human beings could never be lost, for they were always with their kin, and the Paleolithic mind was therefore necessarily in its element wherever it happened to find itself. (p. 13)

The Paleolithic mind "regarded nature as intrinsically feminine" (p. 12). This essentializing claim hinges on Oelschlaeger's use of the Magna Mater metaphor (which he distinguishes from the Earth Mother of Neolithic fertility cults). Magna Mater, the Great Mother, though not a conscious object of belief for the primitive, metaphorically rests on

> an obvious analogy to females generally, and the human female especially, in nurturing the young, and in the mysteries of menstruation, gestation and lactation. (p. 18)[20]

The manner in which nature is both gendered and sexed here is startling. It is difficult not to see this as a repetition of the male phantasy of feminine power, only this time under the name of a postmodern "paradigm." It seems a reasonable implication of this that the feminine becomes a natural principle, and women as category, its representatives. And although Oelschlaeger's response to the existence of critical feminist practice is well beyond that of many other deep ecologists, there is still a sense in which the anthropological space of Magna Mater becomes normalized and inscribed on the female body. Even amidst his repudiation of language as the "mirror of nature," Oelschlaeger is still engaged in the same manner of "epistemological conquest" that seeks new, and ecologically adequate conceptions of reality. Oelschlaeger goes on to make the claim that the Paleolithic primitive thought of nature as alive. Since "the Paleolithic mind did not distinguish the human enterprise from the natural world" (p. 12), it likely "envisaged nature as alive and responsive, nurturing humankind much as a mother nourishes her baby at her breast" (p. 16).

But Oelschlaeger takes this further. Beyond the metaphorical connection between earth-as-mother and woman-as-mother, he imagines that the Paleolithic mind assumed that the entire world of plants and animals, and even the land itself, was sacred. Oelschlaeger quotes Eliade:

> [N]ature is never only "natural," it is always fraught with a religious value. . . . It is not simply a sacrality *communicated* by the gods, as is the case, for example, with a place or an

object consecrated by the divine presence. The gods did more; *they manifested the different modalities of the sacred in the very structure of the world and of cosmic phenomena. . . .* The cosmos as a whole was an organism at once *real, living,* and *sacred*; it simultaneously reveals the modalities of being and of sacrality. (p. 20)

The Paleolithic mind is thus likened to *Homo religiosus.* Yet the possible meaning(s) of the sacred, are left unexamined. The attempt though, is to move the primitive existence into an opposition with what is characterized as the secular character of modernity. Interaction with the sacred was undertaken through metaphorical acts of ritual; cave art is given as the foremost expression of this. Oelschlaeger sees in cave art both the evidence of a belief in a time that is a synchronous, perpetual present, and the dawning of self-consciousness through the ritual inscription of the relationship between humans and the sacred; the cave wall, he imagines, is taken to be the vaginal wall of Magna Mater.

The cave can be interpreted as the vagina of the earth or as the containing space in the earth metaphor of the mother goddess. Its tunnel-like entrance represents a birth canal, and the larger rooms are the womb of the Magna Mater. The setting of the cave, painting, and flickering fire provide a stage for a microcosmic reenactment of cosmic drama . . . cave art and ritual celebrates the eternal and mythical present, reuniting humankind with creation. (pp. 22, 24)

The cave inscriptions signify the dawning of a self-consciousness of the primordial bond between humans and the rest of creation. Cave painting is given as evidence of the need to celebrate and symbolically reenact the miracle of existence in an Oedipal drama of transubstantiation.

Through this ethnographic frame Oelschlaeger constructs an image of Paleolithic culture. A privileged figure emerges from his wilderness; a solitary and deeply connected figure. A human, but not a human. Dwelling in a natural and pristine subjectivity, the Paleolithic primitive is the original ecological subject, celebrating the cosmic spectacle through self-reflexive acts of ritual and art.

Oelschlaeger takes his primitive ethnographic subjects out of the structuring gaze of *the modern mind* and puts them back where he imagines them to belong: in the Garden. And as with most Garden stories, there is a Fall. The Fall in this case happens somewhere in the early Neolithic. The cause: sedentary agrarian culture.

> No one knows for certain how long prehistoric people existed in an *Eden-like condition* of hunting-gathering, but 200,000 years or more is not an unreasonable estimate for the hegemony of the Great Hunt. Even while humankind lived the archaic life, clinging conceptually to the bosom of the Magna Mater, the course of cultural events contained the seeds of an agricultural revolution. (p. 24, italics mine)

This "agricultural revolution" seems to be correlated with an increase in population, and there is an assumption that agriculture presupposes a surplus economy on the level of acquisitiveness. But even without the shift to agriculture, Oelschlaeger supposes that human nature itself played a decisive role in the shift away from the Garden.

> The fires on the caves of our proto-humanoid ancestors presage the retort and the internal combustion engine, just as wooden spears and rock knives portend spaceships and scalpels. (p. 27)

This is a most startling example of a technological determinism at work. There could be no escape for the hapless primitive. Seeking to avoid the lens of history, Oelschlaeger opts for an equally historical lens of progress; somewhere in the telos of the fire there is a nascent NASA. Once the fire was set, the primitive was hailed into a structuring and constituting relationship with technology; the Fire in Oelschlaeger's story replaces the Apple in more familiar versions. But not satisfied with a simple technological determinism, Oelschlaeger makes a similar move to Evernden's idea of humans as misfit/exotic: humans could not help but pick the fruit of knowledge, to start the fire of alienation; "we" were intrinsically, genetically predisposed to be cast from the Garden:

> [T]he human animal is one of nature's mistakes and we are "misfits" in the larger scheme of things. . . . [T]he "big brain" itself is defective. From this point of view the agricultural revolution is simply a pathological manifestation of an inherently flawed human nature. (p. 26)

So whether cultural or genetic, a relentless determinism was at work. Either by virtue of opposed thumbs and a defective brain, or by turning the Garden into a garden, or by seeking the warmth of a fire, the Fall was inevitable and decisive. Humans passed from nomadic, egalitarian innocence, to become warring, authoritative, agricultural and economic agents.

Wilderness, on this account, is created the moment there is a place to call "home." To have a location one calls "home" is to conceptually require a place that isn't. Settlement—to have a place where one is settled—constructs wilderness, and the resultant boundary becomes a highly charged epistemological zone that marks the *inside* from the *outside*.

Hans Duerr, in an extraordinary book called *Dreamtime: Concerning the Boundary between Wilderness and Civilization*, undertakes an investigation of this boundary zone, and of the shifting ways in which this boundary has been constructed between humans and wilderness. He invokes the metaphor of the "fence" to delimit this zone between wilderness and civilization.[21] However Duerr's conception of this boundary zone is very different from Oelschlaeger's. Duerr talks about archaic cultures as having a complex relationship with wilderness such that they self-fashioned themselves through experience of both sides of the boundary/fence.

> In contrast to our own culture, the societies possessing what we call "archaic" cultures have a much clearer idea about the fact that we can *be* only what we are if at the same time, we are also what we are *not*, and that we can only know who we are if we experience our boundaries and, as Hegel would put it, if we thus cross over them.[22]

Duerr's concern is to problematize the fence both for contemporary civilizations, and for our representation of its meaning for archaic cultures; how "we" represent the archaic tells more about us than it does about "them." He argues that modern (Western) civilization has lost a knowledge of events and practices which archaic cultures organized around the boundary zone:

> Civilization, becoming increasingly complex, lost the knowledge of these events. It encountered the things of the other world by inhibiting, repressing and later by "spiritualizing" and "subjectivizing" them. Here lies the root of all "theories of projection.". . . *That which was outside, slipped to the inside,* and if on occasion it was unable to deny its original

character, it was integrated into subjectivity as being that which was "projected". "Nothing is allowed to be outside anymore, since the mere conceptualization of the outside is the true source of anxiety."[23]

Duerr's description here begins to resonate with the move to the outside as I have outlined it. "Nothing is allowed to be outside anymore."

Oelschlaeger sees the fence itself as a heretical construction. A construction that the posthistoric primitive would tear down. The prohibition is thus inverted, and rendered against the inside. But is it really the inside that is being challenged here? Is the posthistoric primitive attempting to un-make civilization, or is the operation here really an attempt to reclaim everything in the name of wilderness? It seems to me that the undoing of the disjunction between wilderness and civilization, by erasing the boundary zone, in a way completes the project that it attempts to thwart. If the outside contains us, then how can it be the outside anymore? By enlarging our precinct, strangeness is relocated to home, and thus neutralized. The complexity of Duerr's elaboration of the function of the boundary is lost in Oelschlaeger's wish to ensure the very possibility of a wilderness to negotiate. Faced precisely with the threats to the existence of wilderness as a physical space, Oelschlaeger imagines a tactic of return, and a strategy of salvation.[24]

The boundary that Duerr describes is an epistemological zone of self-fashioning; Oelschlaeger quotes Duerr's argument on this very point. But he misconstrues Duerr to mean that wilderness conveys the immediate reality of *being human*; as though we would go to the wilderness to somehow *witness ourselves*. The expectation is that we are everywhere to be observed. I read Duerr to say something quite different. Duerr says that wilderness is a place that is visited at great cost; to truly *go native*, to confront another form of life, to be on the other side of the fence, is perhaps also to give up much of the insight which we now possess.[25] But to understand more deeply the meaning of the boundary, to attempt to experience the strange, we need not *become* the strange; we need only incur the risk of comprehending it.

> [N]ot being able to understand the other person, is not a hindrance to, but rather a prerequisite for understanding the strange.[26]

In this sense Duerr advocates understanding this boundary zone as both arbitrary and necessary. The Other which it delimits can function either in the asymmetrical opposition that Oelschlaeger supposes, as separating the good from the evil, or it can be a site that poses questions concerning what the other subjectivities of humans and nonhumans might be about.

Thus there is an interesting kind of tension between Oelschlaeger and Duerr. For the former, wilderness is a project of retroactive recovery, it is an amniotic zone within which dwells authenticity. For the latter, wilderness is the threat of utter loss (that is, from the point of view of identity). It marks a kind of reflective limit in which humans may bear witness to strangeness, to otherness. The difference consists in that for Oelschlaeger wilderness is where we find ourselves, while for Duerr it is a place where we encounter Otherness, and thereby come to know ourselves. We have, therefore, at least two very different sets of operations which take place at this zone that concerns wilderness. On the one hand, a wilderness imaginary, a renunciation of otherness, and a mirror in which "we" are reflected back. And on the other hand, a wilderness-as-other, a radical alterity, which stubbornly refuses to reflect back anything at all. I will not at this point attempt to sort out this nexus between the interiority of authenticity, and the exteriority of the strange. For now we must concern ourselves with the boundary zone, the fence, for it is here that we can begin to see what other stakes are involved.

Going over the Hill

Trinh T. Minh-ha, writing from the register of Third-World woman, feminist academic, filmmaker, and theorist, a multiple other, indicates the political stakes involved in generating knowledge of those denizens of the fence region. The outsider, the "one in need of representation," she says has changed shape according to "our" needs; the common feature being the outsider as the-one-who-needs-help. The aboriginal other has taken on the successive forms of barbarian, the pagan, the infidel, the native, and more recently, the underdeveloped. The ethnographic desire is somehow to make the other the same, without losing the relative position of power. She writes:

> The *proper* anthropologist should be prevented from "going over the hill," should be trained for detachment in the field if he wishes to remain on the winning side.[27]

To go over the hill, to use Minh-ha's metaphor, to incur the risk of comprehension, involves "a suspension of language, where the reign of codes yields to a state of constant non-knowledge."[28]

> Trying to find the other by defining otherness, or by explaining the other through laws and generalities, is as Zen says, like beating the moon with a pole, or scratching an itching foot from the outside of a shoe.[29]

Minh-ha's critique of anthropological positionings is situated much closer to Duerr (obviously) than Oelschlaeger. But if Duerr's claim is that understanding is possible, that the strange may be apprehended, Minh-ha would append the question: What is it that you really want, wanting to know me? To which Duerr might respond, By knowing you I seek to understand myself, but I realize that if I really know you I can never actually *be* myself again. Whereas Oelschlaeger's response would be: By knowing you I seek to recover myself, because I *was* you.

It seems to me that Oelschlaeger's wilderness commitments foreclose any radical insights into this zone of the other—whether that means natives, women, Third world or Yosemite. With the—or, more accurately, "our"—origin firmly placed within an ethnographic and historical narrative, an ontotheology mapping the history of our displacement, Oelschlaeger moves from the "Eden-like" conditions of the Paleolithic through the Middle Ages to the Enlightenment, noting along the way the rise and fall of the Church, the vision of a nurturing Earth giving way to the notion of a divinely ordained clockwork, the rise of capitalism and liberalism, the becoming-resource of the natural world, and, the appearance of countervailing, oppositional voices to modernity. This sets the stage for Oelschlaeger to summon the current canon of American nature writing: Thoreau, Muir, Leopold. It is with an astonishing regularity that American (read, United States) wilderness theory tracks this same ground. In *Wilderness and the American Mind*, Roderick Nash invokes the same three authors as grounding the contemporary idea of wilderness. As does Donald Worster in *Nature's Economy: A History of Ecological Ideas*. But we shall defer directly approaching the American wilderness literary canon in favor of exploring more fully the ethnographic authority which constructs our primitive cultural precursors.[30]

There are several ways in which we can further explore the figure of the primitive and its *mise en scène*, wilderness. From the point of view of the ethnographic claims, we could look to radical ethnographers and critics of ethnography such as Pierre Clastres. Insights from such theorists can help to demonstrate the oracular voyeurism of the deep ecological trope of the primitive. The radical anthropology of Clastres can help to foreground the colonial foundations of this ethnographic maneuver. It can help to show that the deep ecological dream of the primitive has erred in assuming a Darwinian determinism at play in culture, in assuming a homogeneous ground to primitive culture, and as a result, has ended up with a theory of the primitive that views it only in and through the terms and categories of modernity.

Clastres's objection to the deep ecological primitive would be that it fails to pose questions that don't already presuppose certain sorts of answers, and that the questions themselves conceal a host of ideological commitments that are never quite brought to the surface.

By denying primitive cultures a political dimension, Oelschlaeger specifies a primitive existence that can only be understood in terms of ritual practice in relation to nature. Without allowing a political dimension to these cultures, it becomes impossible to pose questions concerning the nature and exercise of power. And without this level of inquiry, from Clastres's point of view at least, it becomes impossible to understand the key feature of primitive societies: namely the exercise of noncoercive power and its relationship to the formation of a state apparatus. Clastres's point is precisely that the true revolution in the protohistory of humankind

> is not the Neolithic, since it may very well leave the previously existing social organization intact; it is the political revolution, that mysterious emergence—irreversible, fatal to primitive societies—of the thing we know by the name of the State.[31]

But Oelschlaeger cannot pose such questions of the political by virtue of the implicit assumption that the political, and the State are things that are lacking in these societies. The answer to why this is the case is given in the very idea of primitive; these societies are prior to politics and the State. The corollary to this I imagine to be that a true society cannot be conceived independent of a state. The bias that is evident in *The Idea of Wilderness*, and indeed evident in much deep ecological literature, is essentially ethnocentric; but it is so in two senses. The first is that primitive society is conceived as a set of absences. The second is the specter of an invisible hand that moves primitive societies into history, and thus into civilization.

Without attempting to address directly the empirical basis of Clastres's argument, we can say that his position is that primitive societies are structured in elaborate ways to prevent the rise of separate and focused power. The mechanisms for accomplishing this are varied, but the outcome is that primitive societies are societies from which nothing escapes into autonomy over the rest; the exits, as Clastres says, are blocked.[32]

A fruitful aspect of Clastres's work consist in his willingness to situate himself on the fence and consider the questions that Duerr imagines are possible only from that location. Clastres's critical position amounts to a refusal (and critique) of the voice of ventriloquism, and its partnership in representational practices. But Clastres's work is primarily directed at the voice of ethnographic authority. As the primitive is required to do a lot of work for deep ecology, it will be useful to look in more general terms at ways of seeing the function of primitivist discourses.

In general, attempts are made to distance deep ecology from overt romanticist constructions. Deep ecologists are at least aware that the "noble savage" is no longer an appropriate representation. Devall and Sessions seek a reevaluation of the primal, they say, not in order to resurrect the noble savage, but as an avenue for the reappropriation of "philosophy, religion, cosmology, and conservation practices that can be applied to our own society."[33] So we have on the one hand a renunciation of the noble savage, and on the other, virtually the same assertion of the prehistoric as the source of a social-within-nature.[34]

Other theorists of the posthistoric primitive, such as Paul Shepard, have a more nuanced vision of the primitive. Shepard prefers to speak about wildness rather than wilderness, and rather than establishing the uniqueness of the primitive, he is interested in determining the common (i.e., universal) genetic imperatives that constitute the repressed of modern life.[35] Like Oelschlaeger, he sees agriculture—domestication—as the wrong turn that has led the human genome into the cul-de-sac of modernity. In "A Post-Historic Primitivism," he writes:

> Societies and cultures are mosaics. They are componential. Their various elements, like genes and persons, can be disengaged from the whole. Contemporary life is in fact just such an accumulation representing elements of different ages and origins, some of which will disappear, as they entered, at

different times than others. The phrase "You cannot go back" can only mean that you cannot recreate an identical totality but it does not follow that you cannot incorporate components.[36]

Yet the categories "primitive" and "primal" are never subjected to a critical treatment. In their discussion of primal peoples and deep ecology, Devall and Sessions write:

> For the primal mind there is no sharp break between humans and the rest of Nature. Many deep ecologists feel sympathetic to the rhythm and ways of being experienced by primal peoples. Supporters of deep ecology do not advocate "going back to the stone age," but seek inspiration from primal traditions.

There are two principle movements that one may detect in this conception of the primitive. First of all, the "primal mind" is reduced to a single kind; its attainment of deep ecological consciousness is demonstrated in the assertion of an absence of a boundary between humans and "Nature." Secondly, there is the claim that deep ecologists have access to the *being* of primal peoples. The first is a kind of colonial reduction of the complexity and heterogeneity of the category "primitive," the second, a claim to an ecological ethnographic authority by which such claims are grounded.

In one sense, the deep ecologists want simply to direct attention to the apparently more ecologically benign existence of nonindustrial peoples. But far too often the mode of reasoning leads to a kind of construction where, for example, we have an argument that says since ecological destruction hastened sharply following the advent of organized and sedentary agricultural practices, it therefore happened *because* of organized and sedentary agricultural practices—*post hoc ergo propter hoc.* Whereas it is certainly the case that sedentary agriculture presupposes certain kinds of social practices, modes of organization, kinship structures and so forth, it does not, however, seem self-evident that the claim to ethnographic authority to represent the "primitive"—agriculturalist or otherwise—has been demonstrated.

The deep ecologists are operating with a culturally specific and highly generalized notion of the "primitive," and engage, implicitly, in another game of ventriloquism. "The primitive does what we ask it to do. Voiceless, it lets us speak for it. It is our ventriloquist's dummy."[37] The figure of the "primitive" facilitates the creation of a narrative for deep ecology; a narrative that shows us our beginnings, and posits an idealized end. The basic grammar of primitive discourses of the sort engaged in by deep ecology is structured in terms of both difference and distinction. Difference defines an analog or continuous relationship, and distinction defines a binary relationship of opposition.[38]

Elizabeth Grosz points out that while distinctions always rely on an empty space, a lack, dividing its two terms, while difference implies no gap or boundary.[39] These two terms allow us to isolate the nature of the complex relationship between "us" and the primitive, and to see what discourses about the primitive attempt to accomplish.

Difference, then, points to the way in which the primitive is conceived in an evolutionary fashion as "our" beginnings. The figure of the primitive represents "us" in a nascent state. Parallel to this aspect is Torgovnick's term the "rhetoric of desire." The desire in this case is the longing to be *like we were*, to *go primitive*. The desire is facilitated precisely by structuring "our" relationship to "them" in terms of (spatial and temporal) difference. As though we tore ourselves away from the primitive existence, at some crucial point in "our" evolution, in order to civilize ourselves; we made a mistake, and through the lens of history, we can retrace our steps (or at least phantasize doing so) and find our way back to authenticity. And what we may mean by authenticity is defined by our immediate (rhetorical, political) needs:

> Is the present too materialistic? Primitive life is not—it is a precapitalist utopia in which only use value, never exchange value, prevails. Is the present sexually repressed? Not primitive life—primitives live life whole without fear of the body. Is the present promiscuous and undiscriminating sexually? Then primitives teach us the inevitable limits and controls placed on sexuality.[40]

The other aspect of primitivist discourse gets played out on the level of distinction. In this case there is the discursive construction of a boundary zone (an epistemological break) which creates a gap between "us" and "them." The rhetorical strategy in this case is not about desire—the primitive is radically broken-off from "us." Constructing an other on the level of distinction seems to be more conducive to manipulation and administration. Torgovnick calls this register in primitivist discourse the "rhetoric of control." Constructing the primitive as radically apart from "us" gives us the ability to control our representations of them, to construct an exotic world incommensurate with our own; a fearful outside, which, while it may represent our beginnings, is constituted by the absence of the very qualities that make us "civilized." The same procedure, Torgovnick points out, is thinly concealed in patriarchal constructions of women as close to nature; women as other, as feared object that inhabits both sides of Duerr's fence.

In this sense, as Torgovnick suggests, the relationship between the "primitive" and contemporary discourses about the primitive is fraught with the residue of colonialism. On the one hand, the primitive offers a path into our beginnings, a path to escape the failings of modern life. And on the other hand, the primitive offers an image of the outside, of the wild and primal against which the civilized character of modern life is assured. These often contradictory rhetorics of primitivism constitute a set of complex and interpenetrated narratives which Torgovnick follows through a range of diverse discourses from Freud[41] to Edgar Rice Burroughs.[42]

Regardless of whether the primitive is punctuated by difference or distinction, by desire or control, the primitive is about use value for "us." Since control of the primitive is not really much of an issue anymore (the history of colonialism has been particularly successful in this regard), desire for the primitive can be indulged. The primitive has been subdued, and provides in the words of William S. Burroughs, only "a modicum of challenge and danger."[43] And this is where I would primarily locate deep ecology on the plane of primitivist discourse. No longer needing fear to motivate representations of the primitive, deep ecologists, in part to atone for the history of suppression and control, move the primitive directly into the field of desire.

The condition (endemic to modernity) that Torgovnick posits as the site of modern primitivism—and this ties us back into Evernden's conception of humans as *exotics*—is "transcendental homelessness." Torgovnick takes this term (from Lukács), to signal a condition that is

> secular but yearning for the sacred, ironic but yearning for the absolute, individualistic but yearning for the wholeness of community, asking questions but receiving no answers, fragmented but yearning for immanent totality.[44]

But it is more than deep ecology becoming engaged in a kind of nostalgic misreading of primitive culture. The point I want to make is stronger than this, as Torgovnick points out:

To speak of *misreading* societies . . . is to exist in a textual universe in which interpretation can be right or wrong but have consequences only within the relatively confined sphere of intellectual life. But ideas about primitive societies and, very important, the persistent Western tendency to process [for example] the third world as "primitive" have made things happen in the political world.[45]

Identifying the primitive in the way(s) that we do makes a difference. By constraining our vision to see the primitive in only certain ways, our ability to think about ourselves is diminished. Torgovnick's caution is that our sense of the primitive impinges on our sense of our selves, "it is bound up with the selves that act in the 'real' political world."[46] She writes:

In the late twentieth century, whether one uses *primitive* with or without quotation marks often implies a political stance—liberalism or conservatism, radicalism or reaction, shame over what the West has done to non-Western societies or the absence of shame. When we put *primitive* into quotation marks, we in a sense wish away the heritage of the West's exploitation of non-Western peoples or at least wish to demonstrate that we are politically correct. But the heritage of Western domination cannot be abolished by wishing or by typography. In fact funny things begin to happen when *primitive* goes into quotation marks. The first thing is that all other constructed terms—especially terms like *the West* and *Western*—seem to require quotation marks as well, a technique that despite its seeming sophistication ultimately relieves writers of responsibility for the words they use.[47]

The recent move to recolonize the "primitive" is perhaps an attempt to remove the quotation marks. But in doing so, the irony is lost and the story comes to be true. The primitive and the primitive tradition again come to account for our present by being our beginning. All of this marks a kind of longing that becomes displaced and projected onto a cardboard cutout of the primitive.

It is a wish for "being physical" to be coextensive with "being spiritual"; the wish for physical, psychological and social integrity as a birthrite within familial and cultural traditions that both connect with the past and allow for a changing future.[48]

As we become more firmly entrenched in the *posting* of modernism, the Western desire for the primitive has not changed all that much, but what has changed is that we no longer need the primitive to offer a modicum of danger (also historically the function of wilderness and aboriginals). The primitive comes to mark a more pleasant dream of belonging and returning, of coming home after the Fall.

At the beginning of this section I said that deep ecological wilderness has come to be a place that is no longer inhabited by primitives. I want to suggest that the deep ecological position of posthistoric primitivism displaces a primitive or aboriginal presence from wilderness. The deep ecologist wants to become the primitive, wants to go native, and this once again excludes an aboriginal presence. In attempting to rethink the culture/nature distinction that has come to set the stage for a history of cultural domination of nature, and those allied with it— primitives, women, Third World—deep ecology projects a covert anthropocentrism. The primitive, the aboriginal, is simultaneously privileged and denied, constructed and erased. Bordo makes this point clearly:

> At the heart of our wilderness picture, a picture of an erased human presence, is the concealed assertion of that very anthropocentrism against which the wilderness was invoked as a path of immanent escape and transcendence.[49]

To paraphrase Bordo, the figure of deep ecological wilderness conceals a double erasure and a double subterfuge. Aboriginal presence— the presence that happens to have been there for a considerable period—is erased; wilderness does not accommodate a human presence. And further if we consider that wilderness in most of North America is a product of a colonial history of appropriation and occupation, we see that this particular history is denied through the assertion of an empty wilderness. By constructing a genealogy of wilderness as an empty space, the colonizers' presence as well as the aboriginal presence is denied. The wilderness construction is thus permeated with the very domination that motivated its construction as a privileged field. To actually be in this manner of wilderness is to challenge its status *as* wilderness; you are not allowed to be there. It is not particularly far from the popular maxim of *take only photographs, leave only footprints* to what Bordo rightly identifies as the founding of a new Kantian formulation of wilderness ethics: "Behave in the wilderness as though you were not there."[50] Thus the wilderness precinct is not only inscribed as a physical space, but appropriate and accepted modes of conduct within it are also specified; if you are there, you must act in such a way as to deny your own presence—which at least means leaving no traces of ever having been there.

Wishing to both deflect the trajectory of contemporary human-nature interactions, and in some odd way atone for the cumulative effect of Western occupation, deep ecological wilderness philosophers make an empty space through which to acknowledge the transgression of human presence; the piety of wilderness. Bordo shows how the cruciform, singular tree foregrounded in the images of the Group of Seven demonstrates all of these movements: this wilderness is always empty; there is no trace of the presence of the human witness, nor is there any other human presence to be seen.[51]

Part of the argument that I have been making here could be taken to mean that a certain relativistic chasm separates "us" from the "them" of the primitive, and "us" from the "it" of wilderness; the spaces and creatures that we misconstrue with our stubbornly historical representational vision. In a way this is true; but the idea of relativism that I want to suggest is not a radical relativism of incommensurability. I don't think that sufficient effort has been expended on these sorts of questions in order to settle on the radical thesis. Rather, it is a relativism that marks out the limitations intrinsic to any location. What wilderness is, and what "primitive" subjectivities might be are questions that have yet to be properly posed . . . answers are entirely premature. Minh-ha again: What is it that *you* really want, wanting to know me? But somehow these questions must be posed. If, as it seems, the wilderness and primitive of deep ecology turn out to be fabrication and projection, then what is worthwhile in pursuing these ideas? This question is indeed a problem, for if we say yes, we must also commit to developing a problematic which avoids the pitfalls that I have been laboring to articulate. What language would this require? What discursive and nondiscursive practices might be adequate to this task? We can, and perhaps have learned something by critically examining some of the conceptual aspects of deep ecology, but what happens next? This, I suppose, comes down to a question of how we are to represent the current ecological situation. In a sense "we," the big we—humankind—are being hailed by the world to respond to the threats to "our" standing. To date the responses have been varied, but mostly predictable. The move to the outside of deep ecology has been one such response, but the language it speaks, is far too busy with the baggage of its unexamined prior agendas.

4

Boundary Disputes

But does not critique, understood as critique of
knowledge itself, express new forces capable of
giving thought another sense? A thought that would
go to the limit of what life can do, a thought that
would lead life to the limit of what it can do? A
thought that would affirm *life instead of knowledge*
that is opposed to life. Both would go in the same
direction, carrying each other along, smashing
restrictions, matching each other step for step, in a
burst of unparalleled creativity. Thinking would
then mean discovering, inventing, new possibilities
of life.
                    —Gilles Deleuze, *Nietzsche and Philosophy*

Up to this point I have tracked a rather circuitous and idiosyncratic route. From Earth Day to panopticism; from general systems theory to an Earth become spaceship; from empty wilderness to lively primitives; modernity to the anthropocentric circle. My method has been to keep moving, to keep questioning and probing this thing called deep ecology. At times I have addressed deep ecology as a movement as it has been described by writers who would call themselves deep ecologists, and some who might not. At other points I have been considering it as a mood, or tendency, or condition of thought. What I have been attempting to do is show how (in a variety of contexts) an ecology without a critical practice can never be deep. What I have left to do, therefore, can be expressed in the idea that an ecology *with* a critical practice might never dream of depth to begin with.

To set about doing this we must disengage from the negative moment of critique and try to push the discussion into a new zone. This is a zone in which we may come to understand how the problematic of deep ecology must come down to questions of critical practice. Such questions of critical practice are germane not only to environmentalism and deep ecology, but in general to the ways in which any resistance is directed toward socially and culturally coded modes of thought and behavior.

If reversing the privileged pole of the nature/culture binarism accomplishes nothing more than a sleight of hand, differing only in the way that subject/object configurations are specified, then what are the alternatives that don't simply block the way to thinking differently about the regimes of environmentally important terms; I refer here to terms such as "nature," "culture," "wilderness," "environment," "society," "subject," "object."

If we have grown sufficiently uncomfortable with the enclosure of the essentialism offered by environmental accounts, of the desire to find and specify origins, then what other accounts are possible?[1] I have argued that the longing for origins and unity is a trap that provides humans with only an imagined sense of organic belonging. It is imaginary, because of a felt security in the boundaries presumed to separate humans from nature, from their technologies, and from the cultures that they inhabit. The developmental model of history presupposed by this thinking posits humans and their modern trappings as somehow like the layers of an onion; peel back the layers upon layers of history, technology, culture, modernity, and on the inside, at the very center, there can be found the kernel of the real human: the ecological subject.

So, we may ask, What is this ecological subject? Or, more properly, Who? Who speaks as an ecological subject? What manner of subjectivity is being sought? Is this subject embodied? Rhetorical questions. Given that deep ecological literature is primarily concerned with clearing a metaphysical space for a posthistoricity, there is little talk of embodiment. Given that the dream of deep ecology is a nondivided reality, there is little talk of subjectivity. And given that the ecological subject, as it phantasizes its decline into a world without boundaries, is given over to a selfless whole, there is little talk of bodies either.

The modern body, we could say, has become a site of inscription and control. From (at least) the Enlightenment onward the body becomes the site of administration and coding . . . the social body, the deviant body, the sick body, the productive body, the heterosexual body. The body as both material and semiotic; compliant surface and code, object of knowledge and subject of depth. But this is not exactly right. As Foucault has made clear, there are two bodies involved that are in a state of opposition. The first is the body as object of knowledge. But the other body is the body that is the site of the subject which cannot be reduced to an arithmetic of organs. In other words, the two poles of the Cartesian body.[2] We might say that what deep ecology accomplishes is to wish away the distinction between these two bodies, but does nothing toward challenging how these bodies come to be constituted. Yet this is precisely what must be done.

With the rise and generalization of a technologically mediated, and increasingly globalized culture, control over the body has proliferated and deepened. Genetic sequencing objectifies the body as text, microelectronic implants augment the body as mechanism. Rather than circling the wagons and resisting this technical and scientific domination of the body by vilifying technology and resurrecting a story about the sanctity of a presumed natural body (a line of defense that seems implicit in deep ecology), I want to make a "slightly perverse shift," as Haraway would put it. A shift that resists what amounts to a dualistic response to the imposition of technological dualism (by which I mean a dualism that is instrumental in essence). If we have no origin story within which to take refuge, and no telos we are destined to realize (by advance or return), then perhaps the only choice is to take control of the techniques—material and semiotic—by which bodies and subjects are fashioned.

We come to see that the ecological subject is a fabrication, which, in and of itself, is not a dismissal—fabrications are simply as good as they turn out to be. The point is, that as a fabrication, and not (as in the wishful vision of deep ecology), a natural kind or state, we have a certain responsibility to ask what is being fabricated, for whom, and from what.

The ecological subject is essentially a reversal of the modern Western subject. Rather than being always and already *subject to* . . . it becomes the *subject of*; of, in this case, Nature. The ecological subject is *par excellence* a subject extracted, and abstracted from the real conditions of its experience. What I have described as the move to the outside can be framed as an operation that lifts and relocates a contested and confused modern subject from its structured relations to ideology, politics, the unconscious, and so on, to a smooth, noncontradictory ecological space.

No longer a potential site of resistance, the ecological subject is undifferentiated from its context. This subject is no subject at all; it becomes a desubjectified organ of Nature. It is a dream of a posthistorical subject and its pathology is that of a transcendental narcissism (Braidotti). Thus the very notion of subjectivity is imperiled under the phantasy of a natural regime. But note the specificity of boundary operations that are required in order to accomplish this evacuation of the subject. The boundary disputes of deep ecology get settled by shifting from one side to the other. From culture back to nature, from humanity back to human. But these acts of boundary jumping never really challenge the boundaries, only *our* position in relation to them. The boundaries remain intact, but a prohibition is imposed against the side that once held an *unnatural* sway over the other. I want to suggest another way of conceptualizing these boundary questions. An alternative that on the one hand foregrounds and disrupts these boundaries presupposed by the deep ecological subject, and on the other, opens up novel opportunities within which questions may be posed.

To begin with, I want to look at the manner in which the critical practices of Donna Haraway may provide insight toward a critical restructuring of radical environmentalism. She has some interesting things to say about these boundaries that deep ecology requires to prop up its ecological world. Haraway also gives us the figure of the cyborg. The cyborg, as I will attempt to explain, is a lively actor who inhabits those regions once occupied by fixed boundaries; boundaries that operated as the ontological and epistemological guarantors of a neatly divisible world.

Cyborg worlds are not all that strange. For Haraway the cyborg *is* us. It is a manner of apprehending our theoretical and material status in the late twentieth century. It is not bent on nostalgia, or repudiation. It has no home to which it may dream of returning. It is a creature of both culture and of nature. And as such, it can never attempt to make one explain the other; it has as much affinity for technology as it does for wilderness. And the cyborg knows well the danger involved in modernism turned reactionary.

Boundary Games

Let us consider these boundaries that are presupposed and reified for the construction of the deep ecological subject. The essential humanness that for deep ecology both defines "our" real being and links us to our paleolithic predecessors, seems to disappear once these boundaries are questioned. Without the legitimating function of these boundaries we need to look elsewhere for stories to tell about the meaning of being human. And in doing so, we might discover that unimaginable kinships become possible.

Boundary breaches, ruptures in the ontological certainty that determine the ecological subject and the Cartesian subject, are everywhere in evidence from the contemporary Western vantage point. Haraway identifies three key breaches that bear on this discussion; boundary breaches that foreground and subvert a fixed, eternal human story:

- human-animal
- human-machine
- physical-non-physical

In the first case, human-animal, the distinctions that were taken as given have been eroded to the point of complete ambiguity. "By the late twentieth century," she writes,

> the boundary between human and animal is thoroughly breached. The last beachheads of uniqueness have been polluted if not turned into amusement parks—language, tool use, social behavior, mental events, nothing really convincingly settles the separation of human and animal. . . . Biology and evolutionary theory over the last two centuries have simultaneously produced modern organisms as objects of knowledge and reduced the line between humans and animals to a faint trace re-etched in ideological struggle or professional disputes between life and social science.[3]

This breached and confused boundary between human and animal has had some interesting results in the past decades. For example, it has provided an avenue for renewal of sociobiological/biological-deterministic discourses about human animality. The recent sociobiology debate centering on the work of E. O. Wilson and his colleagues is a good example.[4] But Haraway wants to push the boundary breakdown in another direction entirely. She suggests that as the distinctness of humans in relation to animals no longer reflects the security of self-evident difference, the boundary zone becomes a site for political and semiotic negotiation. Haraway sees in this particular transgressed boundary the possibility, not for a crisis in the meaning of being human, but for the fulfillment of pleasurable couplings. Neither is this about the "death of the subject." That the death of the subject proclamations coincide historically with the attempts of women and other others to gain access to speech, writing, and other acts of self-representation severely undermines the emergence of these new speaking subjects; to arrive at a conclusion of the subject's demise is to arrive at the wrong answer to the right question. Dismantling the centered and masterful subject is an affirmative project, ending not in the absence of the subject or its incorporation into the body of nature, but in new and positive conceptions of social subjectivity.

> Feminist deconstructions of the "subject" have been fundamental, and they are not nostalgic for masterful coherence. Instead, necessarily political accounts of constructed embodiments, like feminist theories of gendered racial subjectivities, have to take affirmative *and* critical account of emergent, differentiating, self-representing, contradictory social subjectivities, with their claims on action, knowledge, and belief.[5]

Fundamentally, for Haraway this seems to indicate that the meaning of humans qua organisms is, so to speak, up for grabs. We have therefore an opportunity to contest for meaning(s). It also means, and this points to the political character of Haraway's work (to which I shall return), that the construction of boundaries—because arbitrary, and motivated, and thus both ethical and irreducibly political—implies a responsibility. Boundary-making is a political act. In the absence of stable, eternal and transcendental authorizations for the human/animal distinction, the boundaries "we" make *can* be the result of active and affirmative human engagement in the very act of boundary-making.

Similarly, Haraway describes the breach between the human-animal and machine as signaling an ambiguous relationship between the natural and artificial, the mind and body, and the autopoetic and technological.

> Pre-cybernetic machines could be haunted; there was always the specter of the ghost in the machine. This dualism structured the dialogue between materialism and idealism that was settled by a dialectical progeny called spirit or history, according to taste. But basically machines were not self-moving, self-

designing, autonomous. They could not achieve man's dream, only mock it. They were not man, an author to himself, but only a caricature of that masculinist reproductive dream. To think they were otherwise was paranoid.[6]

Today, however, there is no such haunting.

Late twentieth-century machines have made thoroughly ambiguous the difference between natural and artificial, mind and body, self-developing and externally designed, and many other distinctions that used to apply to organisms and machines. Our machines are disturbingly lively, and we ourselves are frighteningly inert.[7]

Prosthesis, extension (McLuhan), these things presuppose a point of contact, a boundary which is a zone of articulation between a subject and an object, a Man and a Machine. Where "we" end and where our machines begin has come to be thoroughly ambiguous.

In the essay *Xerox and Infinity*, Jean Baudrillard draws out a similar observation. He contends that the contemporary Western world is involved in an ongoing crisis born of the radical uncertainty concerning the status of the subject and object. Modern technology both mediates and facilitates this uncertainty. He asks, "Am I a man, am I a machine?" This anthropological question, he says, has no answer.

In the relationship between workers and traditional machines, there is no ambiguity whatsoever. The worker is always estranged from the machine, and is therefore alienated by it. He keeps the precious quality of alienated man to himself. Whilst new technology, new machines, new images, interactive screens, do not alienate me at all. With me they form an integrated circuit. Video, TV, computer . . . like contact lenses, are transparent prosthesis as if they were integrated to the body. . . . Here, the quality of being human, as opposed to being a machine, is undecidable.[8]

However, where Baudrillard wants to accentuate a subject/object ambiguity by, so to speak, sophisticating the undecidable, Haraway uses that very ambiguity to point to a more basic condition of undecidability. It's not just the idea that today machines are such that the point of contact between "us" and the machine is ambiguous, it's that the wish to construct and reify a boundary is tightly coupled with a commitment to a kind of clarity of thought and vision that can no longer appeal to an *a priori* of legitimation.

The third boundary breakdown concerns the distinction between the physical and the nonphysical. It speaks to the specific character of the machine/organism breach, and the manner in which miniaturization and microelectronics have fundamentally altered our experience of the machine. Today our machines no longer have the quality of being locatable and discrete. The twentieth century machine has become diffused and fluid. While it is now difficult to view technology as an *extension* (in simply an exosomatic sense), it also becomes increasingly difficult to see it as augmentation and enhancement. Indeed, with the developments in biotechnology and microelectronics, and now, the controversial dreams of nanotechnology, it becomes difficult to "view" technology at all. Technology is moving out of our visual field entirely. *Homo faber* comes to be a grossly inadequate and rather quaint metaphor for an increasingly complex and chaotic situation. *Machines can be considered as the organs of the human species*, as Georges Canguilhem has put it.[9]

William Gibson's *cyberspace*—a planetary grid of information and control that is both consensual and hallucinatory[10]—is illustrative of this idea that the point at which contemporary technology attaches to human activity is no longer clear. Gibson's *Neuromancer* could be read as a fictive and horrific rendering of precisely the kinds of breakdowns being discussed by Haraway and others.

The unmediated human body is no longer an operative concept in the not-so-futuristic setting of Gibson's novel. His technological future is not an endorsement of technology as such, but more of a stylistic meditation on the contemporary experience of technology and culture.[11] *Neuromancer* offers a future that is not structured simply on a utopia/dystopia binarism. Rather, it presents the future as a set of possible configurations between technology and humans. But there are no ultimate boundaries, no basic or prior state of being human; the "real" is not set out in opposition to the constructed, or artificial. In an essay sympathetic to the convergence between Gibson and Haraway, Peter Fitting writes:

> The dissolution of the defining boundaries of the human in
> Gibson's work is . . . marked by the electronic (re)production

of the shapes and sounds, thoughts, and experiences of the human. In this futuristic society of the spectacle, people depend on technology to re-present their experiences and perceptions for them.[12]

We will return to Gibson's future, because it represents an important figuration of Haraway's work; important, because it represents a future where the breached boundaries we have been discussing provide a context for the total commodification of "reality."

The claim here is that boundaries have meaning only from particular locations and in particular times. That is, they are necessarily spatially and temporally situated. In other words, boundaries have meaning only for particular, locatable, and embodied subjects. To extend boundary claims beyond the partial vision offered by any particular location is to assume or authorize a transcendental operation, or move to the outside.[13]

Yet on the face of it, there would seem to be something of a dilemma. On the one hand—Haraway's account—boundary claims, knowledge claims, are always situated, and therefore always local. Thus we may wonder how we could engage an ecological problematic that—in a broad context—is decidedly nonsituated and nonlocal. Whereas on the other hand—the perspective of deep ecology—through its construction of a single large context (i.e., Earth), one could claim that there would at least seem to be the possibility of grasping an ecological situation writ large. But through the flattening out of the contents of the deep ecological precinct—the "Earth"—there is simply no way to distinguish the specificity of either the production of ecological problems, nor to disentangle the various ongoing, power-differentiated struggles that may have only a proximate connection to environmental resistance. The problem would seem to imply a disjunction that either one grasps the Earth's condition (and, for example, the place of species within it), or one forgoes the construction of problems as global systems, and grasps the situation only partially, owing to a necessary situatedness and locality. But such a problem is only a superficial dilemma. It is not really a situation of either/or, as though the two options were in simple opposition. The deep ecological position is predicated upon an insistence that the boundary disputes have not taken place. Or if they have, the setting has been only within the aberrant disconnection of the modern mind. The point is that without this founding disavowal there could simply be no grounds for the totalizing operations that deep ecology undertakes. To assert that knowledge claims must always be somehow situated, rooted in a location, a perspective, is not to forgo knowledge, nor is it to undermined the possibility (and necessity) of confronting an ecological problematic. Rather, it is to allow the problem to be thought in all its terrifying complexity. It is to resist the seductive imperative of simplicity. So my interest in Haraway is to consider to what extent the theoretical position she stakes out can help.

The Cyborg Trope

For Haraway, the figure that emerges from these disrupted boundary zones is the cyborg. Created as an ironic and provocative tool to subvert the essentializing and naturalizing tendencies within certain feminist critical practice, the cyborg is a political myth and theoretical apparatus that thrives on both contingency and contradiction.

As Haraway puts it, the cyborg "is a cybernetic organism, a hybrid of machine and organism, a creature of social reality as well as a creature of fiction."[14] In so far as we, today, inhabit a world of concrete social experiences, and of simulation, virtual reality, media events, and globalization, the cyborg offers itself as a metaphor that has no particular allegiances. The cyborg represents the breakdown and radical contingency in the late twentieth century of the traditional beachheads between nature and culture, self and other, gender and sex, subject and object.

But, we may point out, the cyborg is also the offspring of both biology and technology, organism and machine. It is thus also the progeny of militarism, patriarchal capitalism, industrialism, and state socialism. No problem. Haraway simply embraces this apparent contradiction by pointing out that illegitimate offspring "are often exceedingly unfaithful to their origins. Their fathers, after all, are inessential."[15]

Haraway describes the cyborg this way:

> The cyborg is resolutely committed to partiality, irony, intimacy, and perversity. It is oppositional, utopian, and completely without innocence. No longer structured by the polarity of public and private, the cyborg defines a technological polis based partly on a revolution of social relations in the *oikos*, the household.

The cyborg describes a condition in which traditional boundary wars are finally visible as fabrications that have a profound kinship with Western science, politics, and ideology. But it is also a deconstructive figure, because once it is brought into view, all sorts of other discursive maneuvers become short-circuited. Nature and Culture are reworked, she says,

> the one can no longer be the resource for appropriation or incorporation by the other. The relationships for forming wholes from parts, including those of polarity and hierarchical domination, are at issue in the cyborg world.

And from the point of view of a radical environmental position, the cyborg is a sobering reminder and injunction against the deep ecological algebra of nostalgia.

> Unlike the hopes of Frankenstein's monster, the cyborg does not expect its father to save it through restoration of the garden. . . . The cyborg would not recognize the Garden of Eden; it is not made of mud and cannot dream of returning to dust.

The cyborg has a certain resistance to the charge that since it is a techno-organic feature of the contemporary world, it cannot know what has been sacrificed to reach this point in history. To the extent that the cyborg describes a contemporary mode of existence, and to the extent that in various ways we are embodied in this existence, a cyborg politics has no recourse to an imagined organic unity to act as a foundation for resistance.

> Perhaps this is why I want to see if cyborgs can subvert the apocalypse of returning to nuclear dust in the manic compulsion to name the Enemy.[16]

The cyborg itself reveals a contradictory standpoint. Just as the cyborg is about control, and high technology, it is also about the "lived social and bodily relations in which people are not afraid of their joint kinship with animals and machines."[17] As Haraway sees it, for far too long American social and political theorists have based critiques on a nexus between the domination of technics on the one hand, and an organic humanity on the other. To draw the cyborg into a discussion about radical environmental theory provides a ground that is as skeptical of technological optimism as it is of a return to an unmediated organic body; it is as wary of determinism as it is of radical social constructionism. Cyborgs can't return to the wilderness because they were never there to begin with, nor do they dream of an amniotic nature prior to culture.

The cyborg trope requires a kind of double vision; it is about binarisms, but it is also resistant to the urge to construct a single unity—it is a dream "not of a common language, but of a powerful infidel heteroglossia"[18] It is a dream of a strategic, shifting identity. A kind of identity, as Teresa de Lauretis has put it, "that is made up of heterogeneous and heteronomous representations of gender, race and class, and often indeed across languages and cultures; an identity that one decides to reclaim . . . and that one insists on as a strategy."[19]

Haraway's argument for the utility of the cyborg myth is grounded in the conviction that deconstructing the languages of mastery, the doctrines of objectivity, and the "sense" of public truths is not enough. The point is not "anything goes." Radical social constructionism has been a stunningly potent means for showing the nakedness of an imperious objectivity, but it can and must not be allowed to lapse into the play of cynicism.

The basic problematic that she identifies is how to have

> simultaneously an account of radical historical contingency for all knowledge claims and knowing subjects, a critical practice for recognizing our own "semiotic technologies" for making meanings, *and* a no-nonsense commitment to faithful accounts of a "real" world.[20]

How can we account for this radical historical contingency *and* a no-nonsense commitment to faithful accounts of reality? Clearly this asks for a great deal.

I think that part of the answer to this is to be found in a kind of pragmatism, an attentiveness to the practices of everyday living, that infuses Haraway's work. On the one hand she takes account of the historical contingency of what can count as nature, and therefore, in general as an object of scientific knowledge. But on the other hand she is unwilling to dispense with a belief in "old-fashioned science for the people." She maintains a belief that "Enlightenment modes of knowledge *have* been radically liberating; that they give accounts of the world that *can* check arbitrary power," and that these accounts of the world "ought to be in the service of checking the arbitrary."[21]

The knowledge claims that Haraway maintains for her political theory mark a desire for a kind of emancipatory successor science project "and a postmodern insistence on irreducible difference and radical multiplicity of local knowledges."[22] So we have *both* radical constructionism on the level of knowledge claims, *and* a kind of scientific realism. There is no particular transcendence involved here; just the acknowledgment that boundaries and meanings are constructs, and their fabrication speaks more to forms of human agency than it does to ontological certainty; this I would call a form of weak ontology.

We don't want a theory of innocent powers to represent the world, where language and bodies both fall into the bliss of organic symbiosis. We also don't want to theorize the world, much less act within it, in terms of Global Systems, but we do need an earth-wide network of connections, including the ability to partially translate knowledges among very different—and power-differentiated—communities. We need the power of modern critical theories of how meanings and bodies get made, not in order to deny meaning and bodies, but in order to live meaning and bodies that have a chance for the future.[23]

The disruption of boundaries that the cyborg myth foregrounds, is always and necessarily ambiguous with respect to its promise. And this signals a kind of playful heroics of the cyborg. Haraway's cyborg signals not a collapse into some variant of a return, but an advance into the zone of greatest danger. This is reminiscent of Hölderlin's words that propelled Heidegger's thinking on the ambiguity of technology—"But where the danger is, grows the saving power also."[24] Haraway's wager is that the cyborg can find the weak points, the points that offer political possibilities for more pleasurable modes of life from within the planetary grid of technological dominations.

The Wager

The cyborg *is* a wager. The stakes are whether it really is possible to contest for meanings at this moment in history. Haraway believes it is. And so, we could say, do the deep ecologists. Their procedures, though, could hardly be further apart.

In this work I have attempted to show that the search for a single ground of meaning, for a unity of voice, and for an ultimate explanatory practice is an unreflective way to replace dangerous old totalities with equally dangerous new ones. *And the demand is, put something in my place.* Clearly we can say that the cyborg imagery is not about *going home.* It is about reimagining what home might come to mean. But what sort of futures can cyborgs inhabit? William Gibson's high-tech low-life future is one possibility. Indeed, the globalization that has taken place in his future is entirely plausible; the *Neuromancer* future is not separated from us by any radical break whatsoever.

What I find provocative about Gibson's future is that it foregrounds precisely what is missing from the deep ecological future: the body. True, the globalized future he writes about is not particularly pleasant. The market economy has totalized, the technological structuring of the world is complete, and global politics is explicitly about corporate life. The dissolution of political boundaries in favor of corporate structures creates an increasingly homogenized global structure of "the poor." The concept "Third World" no longer designates a region, but a global class. Linguistically hybridized, and inhabiting vast metropolitan zones (e.g., BAMA—Boston-Atlanta Metropolitan Axis), the majority of humans occupy the fringes in relation to the corporate elite.

Technology in Gibson's future is virtually synonymous with commodity. Money can buy a near infinite array of techno-biological couplings. Computer keyboards have been replaced by direct electronic human-machine interfaces. Surgical implantation of a port in the human brain opens a field of "simstim"—simulated stimulation—where humans may alter their brains by inserting software implants (e.g., languages, technological expertise), or replay recorded sensory data (e.g., virtual sex and violence). The technological hedonism (or masochism, depending on one's perspective) implied by simulation-as-commodity, posits a future of consumers where the very idea of the Natural and the Human has become thoroughly meaningless.[25] But ultimately what gives this future its edge is the manner in which technology and the body have converged.

We might compare this to another science fiction rendering of a cyborg future that tracks a slightly different course: *Star Trek: The Next Generation.* Far more subtle and sophisticated than the original series, *The Next Generation* is a posteconomic future of political détente. The gunboat diplomacy and overt colonialism of the original series has been replaced by a gentler and more insidious form of colonialism in which the Other is not simply subdued, taught English and the meaning of democracy and patriarchy. Rather, the goal in *The Next Generation* is the continued expansion of the "Federation" in the name of exploratory progress. Whereas in Gibson's future humans actively augment their bodies with technological prostheses, in *The Next Generation*, the advance in technology is primarily to intensify the scope of technological intervention; the human body remains the site of ineffable human qualities that cannot be directly replaced by machines. The highly advanced technologies of militarism, engineering, and biomedicine are not about enhancing the human technologically, rather they are directed at foregrounding an unfettered humanity. The sentient android crew member is forever caught in the existential desire to *become* human; in other words, in this particular future it is the machines that want to become human, not the reverse. Because the space environment is essentially void of any contact with the "real," the space denizens simulate their needs with holographic representations of desired realities (and realities of desire).

This future is clean, benevolent, sustainable, and (at least) ideologically committed to democratic ideals; in short, in certain respects it meets the requirements of an ecological—though not deep ecological—future. The futuristic humanism of *The Next Generation* takes on its cyborg character primarily in relation to the way that humans meet their needs, but the humanist theme is most clearly articulated through the encounters with the life form known as the "Borg." The (cy)Borg are, like most alien races encountered on *The Next Generation*, a humanoid race.[26] But the Borg represent the ultimate coupling between humans and machines. Reproduction takes place biologically, but immediately following birth the young are coupled with machine implants. The Borg are scripted as the most frightening of the aliens both because of their technological advancement, but more importantly because of the lose of humanness that the Borg exhibit. Indeed, the Borg are marked by a single desire: the acquisition of more technology. The coupling that has taken place in the development of the Borg species is so complete that personal pronouns are nonexistent. As the final and ultimate cost of the human-machine coupling, the Borg as cyborgs have lost the concept of identity, and with it the moral kernel at the center of this particular story of being human. As with many cyborg stories, there is thus a theme of horror: the threat of the body's incorporation into the machine; the threat of the loss of human agency by being overtaken by the *ratio* of the machine; the threat of the body becoming techno-meat.

These two figurations of cyborg futures—one an extension of advanced capitalism into a hightech consumer future, the other, a postindustrial humanist story about the future of colonialism—are futures that are still structured around the polarity of nature/culture. For Gibson it is the breakdown of this polarity that gives his future its horrific plausibility, whereas in *The Next Generation*, it is in the maintenance and safekeeping of this polarity that the future retains its bold colonial promise. Neither future posits the kind of political renegotiation that Haraway hopes for with the cyborg trope. Yet both futures seem to represent plausible technological and political outcomes. *Neuromancer*, a very cynical projection of the current conditions where political colonialism has given way to economic colonialism, and *The Next Generation*, a future where the economic has all but disappeared in favor of a politics of pure negotiation.

Of the two scenarios, *Neuromancer* is far more theoretically interesting. Indeed, one could argue that *The Next Generation*, in its near pious construction of the essential human, is really a material representation of the transcendental platform that I have claimed makes the foundation for the move to the outside. In comparison, the future of *Neuromancer* appears to subvert the possibility of a normative and singular human story. There is no dream of a return to a homogeneous social or physical body, nor is there a privileging of an imagined past. The problem is that the future in this case is a world where the boundary breakdowns are less the mark of emancipatory and creative couplings that Haraway might imagine, than they are of a place where "objective" reality is otherwise simply unlivable. But the point that is of interest here is that these future denizens indeed *inhabit* their technologies. To use the language of Althusser sometimes preferred by Haraway, individuals are interpellated, constituted fully as subjects, through the grid of technologies which they inhabit, and which inhabit them.[27]

The SF stories that I have been using here to look at the idea of the cyborg describe futures that are still structured around a myriad of dominations. This, too, is part of the wager, but only part. Haraway wants to imagine other stories that are equally fictive and real.

She wants to ask how "we"—whatever this turns out to mean—can imagine ourselves as material and semiotic actors. Actors who engage and exploit the weakening of boundaries. In other words, if we ourselves are the products of both technology and culture, or more potently, compounds of the organic, technical, mythical, textual, and political, what novel modes of action can this facilitate? To begin with, to say that organisms (humans and others) are produced discursively, that they do not preexist themselves, is to radically change what can count as "nature." It affords one the observation that the contemporary condition is not about the denaturalization of "nature," as deep ecology would have it, but rather about the particular kind of production *of* nature that has taken place: an astonishing production of nature (and those constructed to be allied with it) in the mirror of commodity and production.

Yet such a move to see nature as essentially artifactual can all too easily be seen as another kind of violation in the same register as other Enlightenment dreams of domination. She notes,

> Haven't ecofeminists and other multicultural and intercultural radicals begun to convince us that nature is precisely *not* to be seen in the guise of the Eurocentric productionism and anthropocentrism that have threatened to reproduce, literally, all the world in the deadly image of the Same?[28]

And this is of course an important intervention. But nature as artifactual, Haraway argues, opens a space where what counts as an actor in the shifting and ethnospecific categories of nature and culture is contestable. Our discursive practices for constructing natural objects and processes (biology, ecology) involve us, our technologies, and other actors as well—not all of them human. Haraway writes:

> Organisms emerge from a discursive process. Biology is a discourse, not the living world itself. But humans are not the only actors in the construction of the entities of any scientific discourse; machines (delegates that can produce surprises) and other partners (not "pre- or extra-discursive objects," but partners) are active constructors of natural scientific objects.[29]

In its scientific embodiments, nature is made through the actions of many different kinds of actors. At this juncture Haraway again distances her project from a position (that she labels postmodern) in which "the world is denatured and reproduced in images and replicated in copies."[30] Such a theoretical position (which amounts to a violent and reductive form of artifactualism) grants agency to only one kind of actor: Humans. Haraway's response is not a transcendental naturalism, but a move to confront the hyperproductionist position (and its corollary, humanism), which always comes down to the story line that

> man makes everything, including himself, out of the world that can only be resource and potency to his project and active agency. This productionism is about man the tool-maker and -user, whose highest technical production is himself; i.e., the story line of phallogocentrism.[31]

In this respect, she aligns both modernism and postmodernism, and claims in distinction, that her (scientific) project is *a*modern. The amodern, or the nonmodern, following Bruno Latour, is an idea that involves the

> retrospective realization that from the beginning of the scientific revolution, we have never been modern. These revolutions have never happened. We have never been cut off from our past; we have never been different.[32]

What this exactly means for Haraway is not to my thinking made entirely clear, but nominally she is making the claim that both modernism and postmodernism (that is, a cultural movement that rebelled against modernity, and a cultural movement less founded on rebellion than on a loss of faith generally) are determined by the ideology of the Enlightenment. To accede to the artifactuality of nature, to its social and cultural construction, and then to pull from the wreckage fully formed categories of society and culture, is to remain within the influence of the contested binary pairs; only in this case, the categories of society and culture are granted a transcendental quality. In this sense, society and culture are being used to *explain* nature. Haraway wants to undermine this theoretical tendency, by attempting a position "where neither culture nor nature can be used to explain the other."[33] And this means either the social being used to explain the falsehood or artifactuality of nature, or nature being used to describe or exemplify the truth about culture.

> When the pieties of the belief in the modern are dismissed, both members of the binary pairs collapse into each other as into a black hole. But what happens to them in the black hole is, by definition, not visible from the shared terrain of modernity, modernism, or postmodernism.[34]

And to this we could add the "posthistoric," and the "premodern." If we consider the way that deep ecology attempts to refigure wilderness and the fetishized primitive, we can see that it is only through the register of the modern that these things are explained. And this is what the deep ecologists have failed to grasp. Even in their attempts to characterize the modern pathology, to show how the register of domination (of nature and others) has become a kind of death drive of the modern, they remain deeply, and blindly rooted within it. In relation to the antimodern, Latour writes,

> Always on the defensive, they consistently believed what the moderns said about themselves and proceeded to affix the opposite sign to each declaration. . . . The values they defended were never anything but the residue left by their enemies.[35]

For Haraway, the amodern is both a vantage point and a critical tool with which she attempts to refigure a science-studies and new practices of critical science. The operative concept being a manner of critical empiricism. Far from foreclosing debates on the location and meaning of boundaries, a critical empiricism is about the always contingent, always dynamic nature of all boundary projects. The kind of empiricism that Haraway calls for is a critical and affirmative antidote to the constructionism/objectivity nexus. It is an empiricism that seeks engagement, sympathy. It engages the world not as a set of particularities to be explained by a preexisting abstraction (objectivity), or as a set of contingencies to be explained only by particular abstract and historical traditions (constructionism). It is, as Deleuze and Parnet have put it, "Neither identification nor distance, neither proximity, nor remoteness, for, in all these cases, one is led to speak for, in the place of. . . . One must on the contrary, speak *with*, write *with*."[36] To "speak with" radically undermines the position of ventriloquism—the representor and the one in need of representation. To speak with the rainforest, or the whales, or the trees is to be in an entirely different arrangement than speaking *for*. It is to enter into a reciprocal relationship in which heterogeneous elements become co-functioning. It is a form of sympathy or symbiosis. And sympathy is "not a vague feeling of respect or of spiritual participation."[37] Rather, it is a way of extracting something new from an encounter between bodies (whether physical, biological, psychic, social, cultural, or linguistic).

Objectivity and Others

Among the fogs and miasmas which obscure our fin
de millénaire, *the question of subjectivity is now
returning as a leitmotiv.*
— Félix Guattari, Chaosmosis

Haraway's political vision concerns the emancipatory politics that can
be imagined within a form of life (ours) that is not neatly divisible into
culture(s), society, nature, environment, and so forth. Knowledge production—scientific or otherwise—takes on a very different and limited
potency in her political analysis. Science and technology cannot simply
be vilified as *part of the modern*, both are tremendously potent means
for making meanings; both are modes of semiosis that when released
from the structuring (binary) principles of modernity hold great
promise. Or at least this is the wager. Everything is about limits, contingency, and responsibility.

> [T]aking responsibility for the social relations of science and
> technology means refusing an anti-science metaphysics, a
> demonology of technology, and so means embracing the skill-
> ful task of reconstructing the boundaries of daily life.[38]

So again, this turns out to be about boundaries and their construction.
It offers itself as a challenge to critically and creatively engage technological and scientific discourses in order to construct meanings that we
can live with. This is not the totalized We of the move to the outside,
nor is it the relativistic We—"a way of being nowhere while claiming to
be everywhere equally."[39] The We that Haraway proposes is a We that
embodies *partial* perspectives.

Knowledge claims that issue from partial perspectives are always
subject to critical interpretation and contestation; knowledge claims are
always a view from *somewhere*—and therefore, are always *situated*.
The kind of objectivity that Haraway seeks, then, turns out to be about
situated knowledge and limited location. Such a proposal could accomplish several things for environmentalism. First of all, it highlights the
problematic kinship between its totalizing moves and other Western
stories that attempt a position of objective disengagement. In other
words, an objectivity of specific and embodied perspective cannot so
easily generate transcendental, normative and total accounts of the

world. It is a form of objectivity that operates in a proximity of involvement, not at a distance of disengagement.

A limited objectivity helps to foreground another problematic aspect of the deep ecological world. It helps to show that the move to delegitimate "modern" knowledge in favor of "primitive" knowledge, or knowledges of the subjugated (e.g., deep ecology's minority tradition) is complicit in exactly the same game. Haraway's discussion of situated knowledges returns repeatedly to this problem of how subjugated knowledges can become discursively legitimized without becoming simultaneously romanticized/appropriated.

> Here is the promise of objectivity: a scientific knower seeks the subject position not of identity, but of objectivity; that is, partial connection. There is no way to "be" simultaneously in all, or wholly in any, of the privileged (subjugated) positions structured by gender, race, nation or class. And this is a short list of critical positions. The search for such a full and total position is the search for the fetishized perfect subject of oppositional history, sometimes appearing in feminist theory as the essentialized Third World Woman.[40]

Her position (like Duerr's) is that it may indeed be possible to see from margins, to see from below and beyond, but the epistemological status of these *other* viewpoints is far from "innocent." On the contrary, they are preferred because they are least likely to allow denial of the critical and interpretive core of all knowledge. She continues:

> [They] are savvy to the modes of denial through repression, forgetting, and disappearing acts. . . . The subjugated have a decent chance to be onto the god-trick and its dazzling—and, therefore, blinding—illuminations.[41]

The question of how to see from these perspectives is obviously far from simple. But, to be sure, it means a refusal of both relativism and totality with respect to "objects" of knowledge. Mapping objects is always a speculative boundary game. Consequently, the claim that Haraway's objectivity makes is not one of detached truth-seeking from some imaginary point above the fray, but of limited, localized, and embodied knowledges. Haraway attempts to shut out the generative logic of the subject/object split by suggesting that the object of knowledge be viewed as an actor or agent (i.e., not objects at all). Her point is that accounts of the world do not legitimately emerge from objective projection onto the world-as-resource, but through a more active and participatory agency between many actors. Accordingly, theory comes to occupy a creative role amongst actors; "the implication is that theory is corporeal, bodily, figurative, not metaphorical."[42] The object of knowledge, on this account, is engaged not through objectification and coding, but through something that appears more like "conversation" bounded by affinity and complicity.[43]

The conditions of such a conversation are that one enacts a certain weakness. One must forgo a position of strength and open oneself to an other. Alphonso Lingis has put this with clarity and elegance:

> To enter into a conversation with another is to lay down one's arms and one's defenses; to throw open the gates of ones own positions; to expose oneself to the other, the outsider; and to lay oneself open to surprises, contestation, and inculpation. . . . To enter into conversation is to struggle against the noise, the interference, and the vested interests, the big brothers, and the little Hitlers always listening in—in order to expose oneself to the alien, the Balinese and the Aztec, the victims and the excluded, the Palestinians and the Quechuas and the Crow Indians, the dreamers and the mystics, the mad, the tortured, the birds and the frogs. One enters into conversation in order to become an other for the other.[44]

Within Haraway's schema it is the idea of "affinity" that allows the cyborg to negotiate its contingent boundaries. Affinity, exposing oneself to an other, can never be accomplished through the distancing operations of objectivity. Affinity in this sense is the agency of the cyborg as it realizes its construction is the porous and dynamic intersection of the material and the semiotic. The cyborg is our ontology, says Haraway, it gives us our politics.

In a brief commentary on the cyborg, Christina Crosby raises some interesting questions with respect to the cyborg and its politics of affinity. Crosby locates the infidel pleasure of Haraway's text in its insistence on inclusion.

> Haraway enlists everything that might make noise, anything that might cause stress in the system, whatever might help disrupt smooth communication.[45]

Crosby's suspicion is that the inclusive scope of Haraway's text may be more about pleasure for the reader—pleasure in witnessing the noise generated by unlikely theoretical couplings—than it is about a workable politics. Crosby's point is that the inclusiveness of the text is an advance made at the expense of specificity. How, in other words, can a cyborg say "no"?[46] Perhaps it is that Crosby's comments are made only in relation to the Cyborg essay, but it strikes me that a wider polling of Haraway's work illuminates a position for the cyborg that is fully capable of uttering a "no". Constructing boundaries, creating coalitions based on lines of affinity, such acts are performative, and as such require agents and responsibility. The very concept of affinity (if it is to be distinct from totality) presupposes something that is different, something that is excluded. So perhaps Crosby makes a move that somehow conflates Haraway's textual inclusiveness with a requirement for political inclusiveness; a move that misconstrues what I take to be Haraway's intention, and in so doing, neutralizes the force of her politics. The only way that Haraway leaves open for determining the "proper limits . . . and boundaries of coalitions" is through a process of contesting and complicity—a complicated and always dynamic political process.

Haraway's thinking on all of this is very instructive. Her approach to the destabilizing of the pretensions and position of the knowing agent is carried out largely via a critique of objectivity. In its place, she argues for situated knowledges; knowledges based not on truth conditions, nor morally anchored to a correspondence between the good and the true. Rather, situated knowledge is always necessarily contingent (or contingently necessary[47]), and determined only along lines of affinity. Within a zone of affinity all manner of affirmative and creative practices may take place. Outside of bonds of affinity, however, the situation is less clear. As Rosi Braidotti puts it:

> One cannot know properly, or even begin to understand, that which one has no affinity. Critical intelligence for Haraway is a form of sympathy. One should never criticize that which one is not complicitous with: criticism must be conjugated in a non-reactive mode, a creative gesture, so as to avoid the Oedipal plot of phallo-logocentric theory.[48]

Ultimately I'm not really sure how I feel about the categorical quality of this moral injunction that criticism must always be in a relation of complicity, although it does seem congruent with Haraway's thinking.

Does, then, Haraway's motivated attempt to facilitate emancipatory political discourses lead one to the point of silence? Where there is no affinity, there is no complicity; how then to speak of others with whom one has no apparent bond of affinity? And what of nonhuman others? What, for example, of the otherness of wilderness?

If one considers the following passage from Blanchot, this problem takes on a new and less troubling character.

> In the relation of the self to the Other, the Other is distant, he is the stranger; but if I reverse this relation, the Other relates to me as if I were the Other and thus causes me to take leave of my identity. Pressing until he crushes me, he withdraws me, by the pressure of the very near, from the privilege of the first person.[49]

On one hand it forces one to consider one's vulnerability, one's own dispersal, and one's own otherness. On the other hand, and this would be a point that Lingis takes up in his *The Community of Those Who Have Nothing in Common*, I discover in the double movement that Blanchot describes precisely a different sense of affinity. An affinity of incomprehension, an affinity that suggests something other than a ground of identity between a self and an other. The distinction Lingis makes is between a depth-perception *of* the other, and a surface-sensitivity *to* the other. In the former, the other is captured (however benevolently) into an understanding, and into an image of thought that requires a kind of thought "that represents the concepts and laws of disciplining, education, job training, professional etiquette, kinesics, linguistics, and ultimately ethnobiology and animal psychology."[50] Such a position, says Lingis, is simply an imperative to thought in order for bodies to act in a practicable field. It is an imperative in the form of an image of oneself that one constructs in order to act in the world—"they are not representations of what one is but advance diagrams of the agent one must make of oneself."[51] This is simply to say that one must order oneself, one's limbs, one's organs, one must order the cacophony of a perceptual field in order to act in the world. I am compelled by this idea because it suggests that there could never be a purely vampiric thought (in a Deleuzian sense); it is always a question of a struggle.

The mode of *surface-sensitivity* to which Lingis refers is in no way opposed to a depth-perception; rather, it commences from the recognition of the same imperative weighing on the thought of the other.

It is to see his position, not as produced by the laws of gravity and his movement, not as effects of physical pressure, but as produced by a representation his thought formulates for his will.[52]

In sensing that this imperative issues to the other as well, that the other makes of herself an ordered surface for the same reasons that I do, recalls in less violent fashion Blanchot's sense of the reciprocity of the other.[53] And simultaneously, it provides a new field in which the question of affinity and complicity may be posed.

When Trinh Minh-ha asks *What do you want to know, wanting to know me?*, she lays bare not only the pretension to the objective and removed status of an inquirer, and not only the countertransferential aspects of traditional ethnographic inquiry.[54] The depth-perception answer is, of course, *I already know you—you occupy a coordinate-space in my psychosocial grid*. The surface-sensitivity rejoinder to Minh-ha is simply *I don't want to* know *anything, I simply respond to your imperative*.

At this point everything has become very complicated. We began here with boundaries of various sorts. I have talked about how thought and theory become destabilized in relation to the absence of stable boundaries. The project of deep ecological theory is subject to conditions no different than any other kind of theory; it is mired in the sway of history. Yet, unlike other forms of contemporary theory, deep ecology is not willing to part with much. To unseat the autonomous pretension of theory, to engage boundary making as an affirmative project, to witness in the figure of the cyborg a contemporary condition, and to see how the decline of objectivity implies a radically different conception of what selves and others and theory might be, in other words, to take any of this seriously, is to undergo a kind of radical realignment with respect to *how one works*.

Critical Weakness: Toward a Weak Ecology

Innocence has been replaced by the ironic mode, induced by the challenge of complexity; my sense of place and position has given way to the uncertainties of an ex-centered voice. Within that limit I

> *acquire a certain freedom. For although the speaking subject may well now be decentered it is certainly not dismissed. On the contrary, more aware of my limits, I become more self-conscious, more situated, more sensitive to my particular place in a differentiated world. No longer able to speak in the name of the "others," to assume their voices and experiences and reduce their histories to mine, a previous monologue spoken in the name of reason, theory, politics or "mankind" (sic) is transformed into the diverse possibilities of dialogue.*
>
> —Iain Chambers, *Border Dialogues*

There is a thematic connection that I wish to interject at this point that connects many of the points that I have been making. It concerns how we might imagine the theoretical strategy implied by the work of Haraway and others. Apart from its playfulness, its lively irreverence, the cyborg illustrates a particular manner of thinking and a certain relation to thought that holds promise for imagining what ecological thought might become. I want to suggest that the critical space inhabited by the cyborg and its implications may be usefully understood in terms of a weakening of thought.

Iain Chambers has written some fascinating pages in the final chapters of his *Border Dialogues*. Through a reading of the Italian philosopher Gianni Vattimo, Chambers takes Vattimo's idea of "weak thought" and attempts to develop its consequences for the role of the critical voice, and its value for evaluating the contemporary condition:

> The Nietzschean scandal resides in the proposal that the surface is everything, that appearance is being, and that therefore the whole dialectic between "appearance" and "reality," between "surface" and "depth," so central to Enlightenment traditions, collapses at a stroke.[55]

Such is the condition of philosophy in the late twentieth century. No longer following the rational course of the unfolding of history, philosophy discovers that there is no Truth against which to set falsehood, no eternal depth to be concealed by an appearance, and no region of authenticity at the end of the dialectic.

Chamber's makes of his invocation of the Nietzschean scandal an opportunity to engage a trend in Italian poststructuralist thought associated with Gianni Vattimo. Through Vattimo, Chambers posits the contemporary condition as one that is not empty of affect, of meaning, or value, but rather, one that is very much alive to the sensation of possibility. The interpretation of the scandal that Chambers wants to develop hinges on reading the decentering of thought and the subject not as a foreclosure, but as an opening. The critical suspicion is that the critique that both exposes and erodes the foundational character of modernity leaves us in a position where we actually are "thus finally free to realize the terrible responsibility of our own her- and his-stories."[56] He writes,

> This suggests a necessary weakening of abstract thought as it dissolves into the languages of a more extensive critical engagement. It declines into a world in which the claims of abstract reason and the search for dialectical identity and the ultimate destiny of history, are pulled up short to be revealed as metaphors. It marks the opening out onto a vista of a more secular, more modest, more fragmentary, and altogether less authoritarian, way of thinking.[57]

The weakening of thought in this sense refers to the weakening of the "autonomous pretensions of reason."[58] This "weak" turn does not imply the absolute death of reason, or the end of value. Rather, its claim is on an always reflexive position with respect to reason and value. It is a kind of thought and practice that must always remain aware of its own artifice, its own locality, and its always limited scope.

What Chambers seeks in his valorization of Vattimo's weak thought is not the end of anything except finality and totality, wholeness and authenticity. His text revels precisely in a proliferation of meanings and bodies, values and possibilities that coincide with the breakdown of modernity's certitude. Like Haraway, Chambers celebrates the novel opportunity to become engaged in contesting for, and making new meanings. The decentering of the masterful Cartesian subject does not deny subjects as such, but rather, affirms subjects as subjects-in-process.

Weak thought is the becoming-weak of thought in the wake of the disintegration, and undermining of the strong, normative, foundational and metaphysical narratives of modernity.[59] Giovanna Borradori notes that the specificity of weakness is "its effort to make operative in a constitutive function, the self-awareness of the impossibility of a 'definitive farewell' to reason, of the impossibility of a radical overcoming of the nexus between rationality and hegemony upon which . . . the whole of Western metaphysics is based."[60]

> The use of the adjective "weak" thus refers to the necessity for reason to operate within a dimension of light and shade, within the chiaroscural, discontinuous, and indeterminate space . . . [I]t refers to the nature of truth at the point in time it lost, definitively, the characteristics imparted to it by the sphere of metaphysical "evidence."[61]

This is a key point. And this it seems is where the Italian stream of thought differs significantly from (American interpretations of) French poststructuralism and deconstruction. Chambers points this out via Vattimo's charge to Lyotard, but I think it is worth emphasizing. Vattimo would claim that in fact Lyotard's celebrated declaration/ proclamation of the end of *les grands récits* is simply another *grand récit.*[62] Not, however, in the trivial sense of Lyotard's self-inconsistency (to claim that there are no total claims has a problematic circularity), but in the sense that Lyotard still appeals to an historical horizon of legitimation in arguing that the metanarratives have dissolved, thus implicating him in the theoretical/philosophical maneuvers he sought to challenge. It is not my interest to get involved in this particular dispute; the point I wish to draw out is that Vattimo is positioned quite differently than many of his poststructural/postmodern brothers in France.

The task of weak thought is to resist the urge to ultimately confute its history, and its metaphysics. Its task is to resist emplacement into the trap set by rationality—the position of strong theory; to repeat, it must, says Vattimo, resist the urge to substitute "a new truth for an old error." This means that the project of "overcoming modernity" consists precisely not in the proclamation of its demise, but, paradoxically perhaps, by returning to it.

> The only way to overcome the metaphysical nihilist tradition is to run along it again, to re-experience its contradictions, to re-write it.[63]

The search for the postmetaphysical is only to be found by "accepting it with resignation, as a sort of illness whose traces we still bring in ourselves."[64] The sort of recollection or rethinking (*Andenken*) that Vattimo calls for is a kind of archeological recollection that deprives history of its authoritative character and so distorts it.

Vattimo captures this sense of a resignation together with a distortion, with the term *Verwindung*. This moves into difficult terrain, an area that Vattimo clearly shows his "strength," but for our purposes here *Verwindung* is the term used by Heidegger against the classic Hegelian dialectical synthesis—*Aufhebung*.

> *Verwindung* indicates a going beyond that is both acceptance [or resignation] and a deepening, while also suggesting both a convalescence, cure or healing, and a distorting or twisting.[65]

Accordingly, the relationship between the post-metaphysical and the metaphysical is a manner of *Verwindung*, and so, says Vattimo, is the relationship between postmodernity and modernity. Vattimo invokes this concept to describe not only modernity, but also "the political 'chances' of postmodern culture."[66]

All of this of course puts theory into a difficult position. To resist manifesting itself as truth, it must reorganize its relations to its own history; and it must do so not through negation, confutation or disavowal. For Vattimo,

> Rationality must de-potentiate itself, give way; it should not be afraid to draw back toward the supposed area of shadow, it should not let itself be paralyzed by the loss of the luminous, stable, Cartesian point of reference. "Weak thought" is thus certainly a metaphor and, to some extent a paradox. . . . [I]t points out a path, it indicates a direction of the route; it is a way that forks from the no matter how masked hegemonic rationality [*ragione-dominio*] from which, nevertheless, we all know a definitive farewell is impossible.[67]

It may be, as Mary Ann Doane argues, that this is not enough, that the cyborg as the privileged figure of transgressed and weakened boundaries is inadequate to the task that I imagine for it. Doane wonders how the cyborg can resist when the very boundaries that it inhabits and dualisms that it resists are no longer in place.[68] But Doane's objection is contingent on reading Haraway as writing from a *post*modern position, a position from which—as I described above—she quite clearly distances herself. Haraway's refusal to situate her project within the postmodern/modern nexus makes her claim a weak one. What is weakened is the transcendental authorization for boundary games as projects of strong ontology. What has come to light is not the absence of dualisms and boundaries, as Doane imputes to Haraway, but the recognition that the structures (political, ideological, historical) that legitimate them are arbitrary. The figure of the cyborg inhabits these persistent boundaries which remain as vestigial structures, stripped of their ahistorical self-presence, but nonetheless manifest in social and cultural productions. While Doane acknowledges a limited efficacy for the cyborg to the extent that "we are still haunted by the old dualisms,"[69] she nonetheless sees this promise as operating in spite of Haraway's intentions:

> These dualisms have not simply disappeared much as theories of postmodernism would like them to. The postmodern culture described by Haraway is still resisted on the grounds of the old dualisms and their maintenance. It would be more appropriate to speak of the overlap and strategies which might be appropriate to such an overlap. *There is no clean break.*[70]

But this I take to be precisely the point. The cyborg needs the oppositions within which it is manifested, and to which its strategies of resistance are directed. The cyborg stands in similar relation to its boundaries as the incest taboo did—for Lévi-Strauss—to the culture/nature dualism. Lévi-Strauss called the incest taboo a "scandal"—the great answer for which there is no corresponding question—because it could not be accounted for within the given terms of nature and culture. (Conceived of as universal, one would call it "natural," but given that it is also a normative prohibition, one would call it "cultural.") At the same time, it maintains its scandalous character only within the nexus of those terms. Writing of Lévi-Strauss's discovery of the scandalous fact, Derrida observes that this scandal is something that no longer tolerates the nature/culture opposition, but simultaneously, it is something that seems to require the predicates of nature and of culture.[71]

The larger context of Derrida's text is that there is no outside of metaphysics from which to operate.

> There is no sense in doing without the concepts of metaphysics in order to shake metaphysics. We have no language— no syntax and no lexicon—which is foreign to this history;

we can pronounce not a single destructive proposition which has not already had to slip into the form, the logic, and the implicit postulation of precisely what it seeks to contest.[72]

The strategy then, and the strategy that Derrida attributes to the work of Lévi-Strauss, involves a double movement: preserving concepts (oppositions), while simultaneously denouncing their limits and contesting their truth value; *Verwindung*, recollecting, and distorting. The critical operation itself being a form of bricolage (using the means at hand), and it consists in

> conserving all these old concepts within the domain of empirical discovery while here and there denouncing their limits, treating them as tools which can still be used. No longer is any truth value attached to them; there is a readiness to abandon them, if necessary, should other instruments appear more useful. In the meantime their relative efficacy is exploited, and they are employed to destroy the old machinery to which they belong and of which they themselves are pieces.[73]

Let us say then that the cyborg is in its way another scandalous fact. Conceived of as a universally augmented human, one would call it natural. But conceived of as a production of capitalism, industrialism, and so on, one would call it cultural. Yet it is only through the assumption of the distinction *between* culture and nature that the problem arises.

This is the strategy of the cyborg: its transgressive character is retained only in relation to the boundaries it challenges. It does not dream of a metalanguage. Such a dream would be a longing for a position of strength, a position above and beyond. Nor does it dream of Utopia: *Ou topos*, literally *no place*. It is, instead, intolerant of the oppositions which structure its boundaries, while simultaneously it requires those boundaries for its political and transgressive character. Since it is structured, founded, through the depth of the traditions, categories and oppositions (culture/nature, human/machine, physical/nonphysical) that it contests, it cannot seek salvation through a return to these traditions.

What can be said of a weak ecology, or an ecology of weakness? I would like to suggest that the important distinction offered by these (less than aesthetically pleasing) terms lies both inside and outside of the two poles of the concept of depth (the deep and the shallow). It is "inside" to the extent that it cannot, through either force of will or strength, overcome the traditions which establish this nexus. But it is also "outside" in that it is an acknowledgment of a freedom afforded by the decline of metaphysical certainty.

The awkward line I have drawn through Haraway, Latour, Gibson, Lingis, Braidotti, Vattimo, and Derrida, begins to suggest a shift in thought that is precisely a way to deflect the autonomous pretensions of reason. For what we discover is that at the very moment when the culture/nature distinction is radically destabilized, so too are its distinctive cohorts—self/other, sex/gender, man/woman. The key word however, is "destabilized," not destroyed, but rendered radically suspect. The idea of weak strategy is but the critical feature of this destabilization. A weak ecology is thus operative and self-critical. It is not bound by traditional oppositions, yet it is born of them. To paraphrase Derrida, it bears within it the necessity of its own critique. What gives a weak ecology its distinctive character is that from its self-critical position it can produce possibilities not imaginable from the positions of the shallow or the deep. The agency implied by a weak ecology consists in working through the softness and fluidity of boundaries in order to reconstruct lives and meaning, identities and affinities, that make for a future of possibility.

A weak ecology provides a kind of theory that requires bodies and locations. It positions theory within an ethics of responsibility, of care. It is an acknowledgment that to say *there are only perspectives* is not to deprive subjects of knowledge, rather, it speaks to the ethics involved in claiming to any perspective. In other words, it is a manner of remaining constantly aware of the responsibility implied in the production of any knowledge. It is not about the perversity of truth, but the complicity of agreement.

The idea of an ecology of weakness offers a direction that resists both the panoptic ecologizing of the world, and the nostalgic restoration of the Garden/wilderness. Such options are but the refuge of the polarity of depth.

We may ask how it is that our desire to contest and rework the boundaries that have now entered a permanent crisis of legitimation will really make a difference in "our" lived, political world. After all, from this point in the twentieth century, dystopic futures (from the Turing-test doubles of *Blade Runner*, to the desubjectified unity of the

"Borg," to the moral ambivalence of *RoboCop*, to the maternal/night-mare other of *Alien, et al.*) seem all too easy to imagine. Yet whatever we might have to say about the sensations (pleasurable or otherwise) afforded by these futuristic images/texts, they represent the contingency and uncertainty of a continued human presence.

We might also ask if, in the end, it is a luxury of the strong to even imagine a strategy of weakness. This seems like an important question, but the answer to this will have to remain open. For the present I am more interested in how weakness can enable a manner of thinking and acting that is not founded in a model of depth.

The weak ecological intervention consists in affirming lines of affinity, of making new coalitions, among a worldwide network of actors and agents. The last thing we need at this point in history is to undergo yet another round of the suppression of difference in the name of the Same. A weak ecology is a hedge against the retro-futuristic moves of an ecology of depth. It is savvy to the tricks of a reactionary ecology, an ecological algebra of reversal, an ecology blind to its own remainder. It resists the temptation of *speaking for the trees*; preferring, as it does, the frame of a conversation to that of a beneficent ventrilo-quism. Its thinking is both/and, not either/or. It selects and problema-tizes. It lives its contradictions, not in the deferred hopes of simplicity, but in the knowledge that complexity is the only game in town. It is not impressed by those who would make a normative distinction between theory and practice, as though theory were simply a signifier for some-thing else. For a weak ecology theory *is* practice, and vice versa. It is, as Foucault has put it, "an activity conducted alongside those who strug-gle for power, and not their illumination from a safe distance."[74] To which Deleuze replied "Precisely. A theory is exactly like a box of tools."[75]

I won't offer any conclusions apart from the hope that there are some for whom this will have made a difference. That there are, in other words, some tools that might be of use in thinking a path through the tangle of ecological threats that are omnipresent on the horizon of the millennium. Tools that are neither deep nor shallow, but critical, complex, embodied, and weak.

Notes

Introduction

1. See Michel Foucault, "Nietzsche, Marx, Freud," *Transforming the Hermeneutic Context: From Nietzsche to Nancy*, ed. G. Ormiston and A. Schrift (Albany: SUNY, 1990), 59–67.
2. "Between marxism and psychoanalysis, which are social sciences—one oriented towards society, the other towards the individual—and geology, which is a physical science—but which has also fostered and nurtured history both by its method and its aim—anthropology spontaneously establishes its domain: for mankind, which anthropology looks upon as having no limits other than those of space, gives a new meaning to the transformations of the terrestrial globe, as defined by geological history: this meaning is the product of the uninterrupted labour which goes on through the ages in the activities of societies as anonymous as telluric forces, and in the minds of individuals whom the psychologist sees as particular case histories." Claude Lévi-Strauss, *Tristes Tropiques* (New York: Athenium, 1974), 64.
3. Gianni Vattimo, *The Transparent Society* (Baltimore: Johns Hopkins University Press, 1992), 40.
4. This list is, and continues to be of instrumental value for me—it is not in any way meant to be canonical.
5. Gilles Deleuze and Claire Parnet, *Dialogues* (New York: Columbia University Press, 1977), 23.

6. Gilles Deleuze, *Difference and Repetition* (New York: Columbia University Press, 1994), 129–32. "When Nietzsche questions the most general presuppositions of philosophy, he says that these are essentially moral, since Morality alone is capable of persuading us that thought has a good nature and the thinker a good will, and that only the good can ground the supposed affinity between thought and the true" (p. 132). For Deleuze, the project of thought seeks a manner of thinking which, like the Vampire, has no image. It is a manner of thinking which opposes itself to a *cogitatio universalis* (Cartesian truth, Kantian just, Hegelian right). This conception of thought, and its formal organization as a general noology, is discussed extensively in Gilles Deleuze and Félix Guattari, *A Thousand Plateaus* (Minneapolis: University of Minnesota Press, 1987), particularly 374–80.

7. Deleuze, *Difference and Repetition*, 130.

8. L. Grossberg, C. Nelson, and P. Treichler, "Cultural Studies: An Introduction," *Cultural Studies*, ed. L. Grossberg, C. Nelson, and P. Treichler (New York: Routledge, 1992), 4–6.

9. Lynn Spigel, "Communicating with the Dead: Elvis as Medium," *Camera Obscura* 23 (1990): 199.

10. Cf. Max Oelschlaeger, *The Idea of Wilderness: From Prehistory to the Age of Ecology* (New Haven, Conn.: Yale University Press, 1991).

11. Steven Shaviro makes this point much more clearly than I can. See *Doom Patrols*, chapter entitled "Foucault," draft copy, electronic text, unpaginated (Seattle: University of Washington, 1995). URL: http://dhalgren.english.washington.edu/~steve/doom.html.

12. Donna Haraway, "The Promise of Monsters: A Regenerative Politics for Inappropriate/d Others," *Cultural Studies*, 295.

1. The Move to the Outside

1. Denis Hayes, "The Beginning" in *Earth Day—The Beginning* (New York: Bantam Books, 1970), 1. Denis Hayes was the national coordinator of Environmental Action, the group that coordinated groups on over 2,000 campuses, in 2,000 communities, and in 10,000 high schools for the events surrounding Earth Day, 1970. This, and the following (italicized) quotes were given (at various locations throughout the United States) to commemorate Earth Day, 1970.

2. Alan Gussow, "The Future is Circular," *Earth Day—The Beginning*, 3–4.
3. Richard L. Ottinger, "Political Pollution," *Earth Day—The Beginning*, 63.
4. Rachel Carson, *Silent Spring* (Boston: Houghton Mifflin, 1962).
5. Paul Ehrlich, *The Population Bomb* (New York: Sierra Club–Ballantine Books, 1968).
6. Garrett Hardin, "The Tragedy of the Commons," *Economics, Ecology, Ethics: Essays towards a Steady State Economy*, ed. Herman Daly (New York: Freeman, 1985), 100–114.
7. Jonathan Bordo, "Ecological Peril, Modern Technology and the Postmodern Sublime," *Shadow of Spirit: Postmodernism and Religion*, ed. P. Berry and Andrew Wernick (New York: Routledge, 1993), 167.
8. François Ewald, "Two Infinities of Risk," *The Politics of Everyday Fear*, trans. Brian Massumi (Minneapolis: University of Minnesota Press, 1993), 222.
9. Bordo, "Ecological Peril," 169.
10. Walter F. Mondale, "Commitment to Survival," *Earth Day—The Beginning*, 47. At the time Mondale was a Democratic senator from Minnesota.
11. Bordo, "Ecological Peril," 169.
12. Michel Foucault, *Discipline and Punish: The Birth of the Prison* (New York: Vintage Books, 1979), 201, 205. Dreyfus and Rabinow put it this way: "The panopticon is not merely a highly efficient and clever technique for the control of individuals; it is also a laboratory for their eventual transformation. . . . In Foucault's terms, the panopticon brings together knowledge, power, the control of the body, and the control of space into an integrated technology of discipline. It is a mechanism for the location of bodies in space, for the distribution of individuals in relation to one another, for hierarchical organization, for the efficient disposition of centers and channels of power. The panopticon is an adaptable and neutral technology for the ordering and individuating of groups. Whenever the imperative is to set individuals or populations in a grid where they can be made productive and observable, then panoptic technology can be used." Hubert L. Dreyfus and Paul Rabinow, *Michel Foucault: Beyond Structuralism and Hermeneutics* (Chicago: University of Chicago Press, 1983), 189.

13. Bordo, "Ecological Peril," 168.
14. Donna Haraway, "Situated Knowledges: The Science Question in Feminism and the Privilege of Partial Perspective," *Simians, Cyborgs and Women: The Reinvention of Nature* (New York: Routledge, 1991), 199.
15. Bordo, "Ecological Peril," 168.
16. Haraway, "Situated Knowledges," 193.
17. Donna Haraway, "Cyborgs at Large: Interview with Donna Haraway," *Technoculture*, ed. Constance Penley and Andrew Ross (Minneapolis: University of Minnesota Press, 1991), 16.
18. Rennie Davis, "Up Agnew Country," *Earth Day—The Beginning*, 87. Rennie Davis was a member of the Chicago Seven.
19. Ibid., 88.
20. William Leiss came to prominence in the early 1970s with the publication of *The Domination of Nature* (New York: Beacon Books, 1972). In this elaborate work, Leiss gives an analysis of how the domination of nature has come to be displaced into a form of domination in which some humans hold power over others with nature deployed as the instrument of domination. In *System and Structure: Essays in Communication and Exchange* (New York: Tavistock, 1980), Anthony Wilden undertakes a breathtaking Marxist-ecological critique of Western epistemology. This book, now out of print, marks one of the high points of modern ecological thought.
21. Joseph Shapiro, "Imperialism," *Earth Day—The Beginning*, 86. At that time Shapiro was associate professor of physics at Fordham University in New York City.
22. Walter Hickel, "Taps," *Earth Day—The Beginning*, 114. Hickel was secretary of the interior.
23. Donald Jensen, "Ideas From Ford," *Earth Day—The Beginning*, 161. Jensen was on the Air Pollution Control Board of the Ford Motor Company.
24. Murray Bookchin, "Toward an Ecological Society," *Toward an Ecological Society* (Montreal: Black Rose Books, 1974), 58–59. See also Steve Chase "Whither the Radical Ecology Movement?" *Defending the Earth*, ed. Bookchin and Foreman (Montreal: Black Rose Books, 1991), 7–9.
25. See Murray Bookchin, *Ecology and Revolutionary Thought* (New York: Times Change Press, 1970), 7–14.
26. Bookchin, "Toward an Ecological Society," 59.

27. Ibid.
28. World Commision on Environment and Development, *Our Common Future* (New York: Oxford University Press, 1987), 40.
29. Ibid. 2.
30. Foucault, *Discipline and Punish*, 206.
31. From the preface to *Panopticon*, quoted in Foucault, *Discipline and Punish*, 207.
32. From the list of principles outlined in the Tokyo Declaration of 1987. Reproduced in World Commision on Environment and Development, *Our Common Future*, 363–65.
33. Murray Bookchin, "Ecology and the Left," *Defending the Earth*, 56. See also "Marxism as Bourgeois Sociology," in *Towards an Ecological Society*, 197–200.
34. Ibid. 207–9. For example, in the "Economic and Philosophic Manuscripts," *Selected Writings*, ed. David McLellan (New York: Oxford University Press, 1977), Marx writes: "The animal only fashions things according to the standards and need of the species it belongs to, whereas man knows how to produce according to the measure of every species and knows everywhere how to apply its inherent standard to the object; thus man also fashions things according to the laws of beauty. Thus it is in the working over of the objective world that man must first affirm himself as a species-being. The production of his active species-life. Through it nature appears as his work and his reality. The object of work is therefore the objectification of the species-life of man; for he duplicates himself not only intellectually, in his mind, but also actively in reality and thus can look at his image in the world he has created. Therefore, when alienated labour tears man from the object of his production, it also tears him from his species-life, the real objectivity of his species, and turns the advantage he has over animals into a disadvantage in that his organic body, nature, is torn from him. Similarly, in that alienated labour degrades man's own free activity to a means, it turns the species-life of man into a means for his physical existence. (pp. 82–83).
35. Ibid. 247.
36. Murray Bookchin and George Bradford have been vocal critics of deep ecology. Both have accused deep ecology of promulgating a deeply naive and misanthropic position. The debate has been particularly heated around the issue of population. Much of this feud

has been played out in the Toronto anarchist publication *Kick It Over*. See also George Bradford, *How Deep is Deep Ecology?* (New York: Times Change Press, 1989).

37. Bookchin has published a great deal over the years, and although I am not particularly moved by his often dogmatic, heavy-handed, neo-Hegelian lecturing, I am always impressed by his critical abilities. His vision of social ecology corresponds to a dialectical naturalism predicated upon the idea that "ecology alone, firmly rooted in *social* criticism and a vision of social reconstruction, can provide us with a means for remaking society in a way that will benefit nature *and* humanity." The challenge for Bookchin is to maintain a critical position amidst the kind of oscillations that swing "mindlessly from one extreme that advocates the complete 'domination of nature' by 'man' to another, rather confused 'biocentric' or anti-humanist extreme that essentially reduces humanity to a parasitic swarm of mosquitoes in a mystified swamp called 'Nature.' We must remove ourselves from an ideological catapult that periodically flings us from fad to fad." Bookchin, *Remaking Society* (Montreal: Black Rose Books, 1989), 13.

38. First published in *Inquiry* 16 (1973): 95–100, reprinted as Arne Naess, "The Shallow and the Deep, Long-range Ecology Movements: A Summary," *The Deep Ecology Movement: An Introductory Anthology*, ed. Alan Drengson and Yuichi Inoue (Berkeley: North Atlantic Books, 1995).

39. Reprinted in Arne Naess, *Ecology, Community and Lifestyle: Outline of an Ecosophy* (Cambridge: Cambridge University Press, 1989), 28.

40. The distinction between ecocentrism and biocentrism is occasionally deployed in arguments concerning anthropocentrism. Biocentrists are characterized as those who privilege the organic but not the human, and ecocentrists are those that seek a harmonious relationship with all things inorganic and organic. This bio-/eco- distinction is the site of an ongoing border war within radical environmentalism, but for our purposes the anthropocentric distinction is held to be necessary and sufficient to delimit the radical from reform approaches.

41. Naess, *Ecology, Community and Lifestyle*, 32.

42. Warwick Fox quoted in Bill Devall and George Sessions, *Deep Ecology: Living as if Nature Mattered* (Salt Lake City: Gibbs M. Smith, 1985), 66. This quote has puzzled me for quite some time.

Did he mean *reify* rather than *perceive?* The only imaginable corollary to this as it stands is: to the extent that we *fail* to perceive boundaries, we slip into madness. Fox's proposal in certain significant respects resembles an invitation to a condition which Celeste Olalquiaga describes (after Roger Callois) as psychaesthenia: "Incapable of delimiting the limits of its own body, the psychaesthenic organism proceeds to abandon its own identity to embrace the space beyond. It does so by camouflaging itself into the milieu. This simulation effects a double usurpation: while the organism successfully reproduces those elements it could not otherwise apprehend, in the process it is swallowed by them, vanishing as a differentiated entity." See Celeste Olalquiaga, *Megalopolis: Contemporary Cultural Sensibilities* (Minneapolis: University of Minnesota Press, 1992), 1–2.

43. Devall and Sessions, *Deep Ecology: Living as if Nature Mattered*, 66.

44. From an unpublished paper by Naess quoted in Warwick Fox, *Transpersonal Ecology: Developing New Foundations for Environmentalism*, 93–94.

45. Fox, *Transpersonal Ecology*, 95.

46. Naess gives a name to his *ecosophy:* Ecosophy T. He does this in order to show that even though the norms he works from are taken to be immanent to organic existence, and even though the process of reflection upon these norms would ultimately and necessarily lead to a deep ecological end point, the *manner* in which he himself develops his own reflections is unique to his own habits and requirements.

47. Naess, *Ecology, Community and Lifestyle*, 38.

48. See Naess, *Ecology, Community and Lifestyle*, 47–51.

49. There are numerous sources where the platform has been published with slight variations. The version I refer to is essentially the same as that presented in Naess, *Ecology, Community and Lifestyle*, 28, and Devall and Sessions, *Deep Ecology: Living as if Nature Mattered*, 70., and Arne Naess, and George Sessions, "Platform Principles of the Deep Ecology Movement," *The Deep Ecology Movement: An Introductory Anthology*, ed. Alan Drengson and Yuichi Inoue (Berkeley: North Atlantic Books, 1995):

1. The flourishing of human and nonhuman life on Earth has intrinsic value. The value of nonhuman life forms is independent of the usefulness these may have for narrow human purposes.

2. Richness and diversity of life forms are values in themselves and contribute to the flourishing of human and nonhuman life on Earth.
3. Humans have no right to reduce this richness and diversity except to satisfy vital needs.
4. Present human interference with the nonhuman world is excessive, and the situation is rapidly worsening.
5. The flourishing of human life and cultures is compatible with a substantial decrease of the human population. The flourishing of nonhuman life requires such a decrease.
6. Significant changes in life conditions for the better require change in policies. These affect basic economic, technological, and ideological structures.
7. The ideological change is mainly that of appreciating *life quality* (dwelling in situations of intrinsic value rather than adhering to a high standard of living). There will be a profound awareness of the difference between big and great.
8. Those who subscribe to the foregoing points have an obligation directly or indirectly to participate in the attempt to implement the necessary changes.

50. See platform point 5 above.
51. Naess, *Ecology, Community and Lifestyle*, 30–31.
52. This rather unusual unit of population growth apparently comes from a UN *State of the World Population Report* from 1984. See Devall and Sessions, *Deep Ecology: Living as if Nature Mattered*, 72.
53. Naess, *Ecology, Community and Lifestyle*, 85.
54. Naess quoted in Fox, *Transpersonal Ecology*, 219.
55. Another more recent variant has been brought to my attention by Henning Braaten, editor of FLUX Magazine in Norway (e-mail correspondence, his translation). Compared to the American version of the platform, this is far less intrusive and authoritarian. It is too soon to measure its reception by the North American movement.
   1. Each individual and all life on Earth has value in itself. This includes cultural life forms. These values are independent of usefulness for human beings.
   2. The life forms unfold in mutuality, with life quality as basis for relationships and civilization. Diversity and richness of life forms are essential for the unfoldment of these values.

3. Human beings are unique life forms. With their ability both to create and to destroy, they have a corresponding responsibility for life on Earth.

4. It is possible and desirable, with respect for all individuals and cultures, to work for a long term decrease of the number of humans on Earth.

5. At present, human interference in the basis of life on Earth is so extensive that it threatens the existence of life itself.

6. A new politics is possible and desirable. A society with quality of life can be built on dialogue and an extended view of the human being, on cooperation and carefulness with the resources of Earth.

7. It is necessary to choose values in direction of life quality, rather than in direction of ever-increasing standard of living.

8. These points serve to awaken for an extended care for fellow human beings and all life on Earth. The responsibility for the necessary changes lies with each one of us.

Although I won't pursue the point much further, I think it is interesting to consider that outside of a very small contingent of (academic) deep ecologists, Naess is seldom referred to in any sustained fashion. Murray Bookchin, Graham Purchase, Brian Morris, and Rodney Aitchtey, *Deep Ecology and Anarchism: A Polemic* (London: Freedom Press, 1993), contains two commentaries on Naess's book. One is favorable, (Aitchtey's "Deep Ecology: Not Man Apart") but critically uninteresting. The other (Morris's "Reflections on Deep Ecology") is quite hostile to Naess's philosophical, formal style. Bookchin's piece ("Deep Ecology, Anarcho-syndicalism, and the Future of Anarchist Thought") notes in passing the "intellectual poverty of the father of deep ecology and the silliness of the entire deep ecology movement" (p. 47). None of these pieces really engage Naess's ideas, nor do they attempt to account for the real theoretical discrepancies between Naess's deep ecology, and its North American version.

56. Of particular interest has been the lively (and at times nasty) debate between the deep ecologists, and the social ecologist Murray Bookchin. A good summary of the issues and ideas at the core of this debate can be found in *Defending the Earth*, an edited transcript of a 1989 debate held in New York City between Bookchin and Dave Foreman, the deep ecologist and co-founder of the eco-activist group Earth First!.

57. A brief selection of works addressing various aspects of the deep ecological movement includes: Richard Cartwright Austin, "Beauty: A Foundation for Environmental Ethics," *Environmental Ethics* 7 (1985): 197–208; Thomas Birch, "The Incarceration of Wildness: Wilderness Areas as Prisons," *Environmental Ethics* 12 (1990): 3–26; Jim Cheney, "Eco-Feminism and Deep Ecology," *Environmental Ethics* 9 (1987): 115–45; Bill Devall, "The Deep Ecology Movement," *Natural Resources Journal* 20 (1980): 299–322; Gus diZerega, "Social Ecology, Deep Ecology, and Liberalism," *Critical Review* 6.2–3 (1992): 305–70; Gus diZerega, "Empathy, Society, Nature, and the Relational Self: Deep Ecology and Liberal Modernity," *Social Theory and Practice* 21.2 (1995): 239–69; Andrew Dobson, "Deep Ecology," *Cogito* 3.1 (1989): 41–46; Alan Drengson, "A Critique of Deep Ecology? Response to William Grey," *Journal of Applied Philosophy* 4 (1987): 223–27; Warwick Fox, "Deep Ecology: A New Philosophy for our Time?" *Ecologist* 14 (1984): 194–200; Warwick Fox, "The Deep Ecology-Ecofeminism Debate and Its Parallels," *Environmental Ethics* 11 (1989): 5–25; William C. French, "Against Biospherical Egalitarianism," *Environmental Ethics* 17 (1995): 39–57; Frank B. Golley, "Deep Ecology from the Perspective of Environmental Science," *Environmental Ethics* 9 (1987): 45–55; William Grey, "A Critique of Deep Ecology," *Journal of Applied Philosophy* 3.2 (1986): 211–16; William Grey, "Anthropocentrism and Deep Ecology," *Australasian Journal of Philosophy* 71 (1993): 463–75; Edward R. Grumbine, "Wildness, Wise Use, and Sustainable Development," *Environmental Ethics* 16 (1994): 227–49; Ramachandra Guha, "Radical American Environmentalism and Wilderness Preservation: A Third World Critique," *Environmental Ethics* 11 (1989): 71–83; David M. Johns, "The Relevance of Deep Ecology to the Third World," *Environmental Ethics* 12 (1990): 233–52; Dolores LaChapelle, "Systemic Thinking and Deep Ecology," *Ecological Consciousness: Essays from the Earth Day X Colloquium*; Freya Mathews, "Conservation and Self-Realization: A Deep Ecology Perspective," *Environmental Ethics* 10 (1988): 347–55; Bill McCormick, "How Deep is Social Ecology," *Kick it Over*, November 1988; Andrew McLaughlin, *Regarding Nature: Industrialism and Deep Ecology* (Albany: SUNY Press, 1993); John Seed, "Plumbing Deep Ecology," *Habitat Australia*, June 1982, 27–28; John Seed, Joanna Macy, Pat Fleming, and Arne

Naess, *Thinking Like a Mountain: Towards a Council of All Beings* (Philadelphia: New Society Publishers, 1988); George Sessions, "Shallow and Deep Ecology: A Review of the Literature," *Ecological Consciousness: Essays from the Earth Day X Colloquium*, ed. Robert C. Shultz and J. Donald Hughes (Washington, D.C.: University Press of America, 1981); George Sessions, "The Deep Ecology Movement: A Review," *Environmental Review* 11 (1987): 105–25; Sessions, "The Deep Ecology Movement: A Review," *Environmental Review* 11 (1987): 105–25; George Sessions, "Ecocentrism and the Anthropocentric Detour," *Revision* 13 (1991): 109–15; George Sessions, ed., *Deep Ecology in the 21st Century* (Boston: Shambhala, 1994); Deborah Slicer, "Is There an Ecofeminism Deep Ecology 'Debate'?" *Environmental Ethics* 17 (1995): 151–69; Gary Snyder, "Buddhism and the Possibilities of a Planetary Culture," Devall and Sessions, *Deep Ecology*, appendix G, 251–53; Richard Sylvan, "A Critique of Deep Ecology," *Radical Philosophy* 40 (1985): 2–12; Michael Tobias, ed., *Deep Ecology* (San Diego: Avant Books, 1985); Alan E. Wittbecker, "Deep Anthropology: Ecology and Human Order," *Environmental Ethics* 8 (1986): 261–70; Michael Zimmerman, "Toward a Heideggerian Ethos for Radical Environmentalism," *Environmental Ethics* 5 (1983): 99–131; Michael Zimmerman, "Philosophical Reflections on Reform vs. Deep Environmentalism," *The Trumpeter* 3.4 (1986): 12–13; Michael Zimmerman, "Introduction to Deep Ecology," *In Context* 22 (1989): 24–28; Michael Zimmerman, "Rethinking the Heidegger-Deep Ecology Relationship," *Environmental Ethics* 15 (1993): 195–224.

58. In reference to the "North American" deep ecology movement, it should be pointed out that the deep ecology movement is essentially a North American phenomenon. With few exceptions—for example, Australians, Warwick Fox and John Seed, and Naess himself—virtually all of the prominent deep ecologists are North American. This observation begs an interesting question: Why has the American ecology movement been far more interested in deep ecology than it has in the mainstream, popular green politics of the sort that we see in, for example, Germany, Sweden, Denmark, and the Netherlands? (The same sort of question would apply to interest in wilderness.) One way to think about this question is to consider that the North American ecology movement is informed

by particular historical and cultural traditions with respect to (for example) wilderness, the land, indigenous presence, the concept of the individual and its relationship to government, and in general the relationship with and to modernity. Utopian thinking, and an essentially arcadian imaginary have long played an important role in the American social and political landscapes.

59. Devall and Sessions, *Deep Ecology*, 7.
60. Ibid., 18.
61. Ibid., 11.
62. Ibid., 67.
63. Ibid., 18.
64. See Gilles Deleuze and Félix Guattari, *A Thousand Plateaus* (Minneapolis: University of Minnesota Press, 1987), 104–6.
65. Gilles Deleuze and Félix Guattari, *Kafka: Toward a Minor Literature* (Minneapolis: University of Minnesota Press, 1986), 19 (emphasis added).
66. Deleuze and Guattari, *A Thousand Plateaus*, 105.
67. Ibid. (emphasis added).
68. See Devall and Sessions, *Deep Ecology*, 18–19.
69. Ibid., 19.
70. Pierre Clastres, *Society against the State: Essays in Political Anthropology* (New York: Zone Books, 1987), 11. Quoted in *Deep Ecology*, 19.

2. Ecology/System/Totality

1. In many cases in the popular literature the terms "ecology" and the "systems view" are used interchangeably. It is unclear to me when exactly the conflation of these two terms began to occur.
2. Cf. Ramón Margalef, *Perspectives in Ecological Theory* (Chicago: University of Chicago Press, 1968), 1–25, for a theoretical discussion of ecological terminology. Good examples of the popular translations of ecological concepts and terms are common, but three that stand out are Fritjof Capra, *The Turning Point: Science, Society, and the Rising Culture* (New York: Bantam Books, 1982), 90–91, 275–85, James Lovelock, *Gaia: A New Look at Life on Earth* (New York: Oxford University Press, 1979), and Barry Commoner's *The Closing Circle* (New York: Bantam Books, 1972).

3. Jean Baudrillard, *The Mirror of Production* (New York: Telos, 1975), 113.
4. Blumenberg's central example of paratheoretics would be the manner in which psychoanalytic theory is capable of turning a resistance directed toward it into the very economy and movement of the unconscious, and thus into a confirmation of a psychoanalytic theory of the unconscious. Hans Blumenberg, *The Genesis of the Copernican World* (Cambridge, Mass.: MIT Press, 1987), 657.
5. See Anna Bramwell, *Ecology in the 20th Century: A History* (New Haven, Conn.: Yale University Press, 1989), 39–63.
6. Ibid., 53.
7. See Bramwell, *Ecology in the 20th Century*; W. Bynum, E. Browne, and R. Porter, eds., *Dictionary of the History of Science* (Princeton, N.J.: Princeton University Press, 1981).
8. Margalef, *Perspectives in Ecological Theory*, 4.
9. Ibid., 17.
10. E. P. Odum, *Ecology and our Endangered Life-Support Systems* (Sunderland, Mass.: Sinauer Books, 1989), 23–24.
11. Ludwig von Bertalanffy, *General Systems Theory: Foundations, Development, Applications* (New York: Braziller, 1968), 18.
12. Ibid., 19.
13. Ibid., 32.
14. Some theorists prefer a tripartite classification of isolated systems, closed systems, and open systems. An isolated system is one which is closed to the input of both energy and matter. A closed system (i.e., the biosphere) is open to the input of energy (i.e., the sun) but does not import materials. An open system is dependent on the input of both matter and energy. See Wilden, *System and Structure*.
15. "A closed system can be defined as follows: It is a subsystem which, by reality or by definition, is not in an essential relation of feedback to an environment. Any feedback relations between variables are strictly internal to the system, or better still, has nothing to do with the matching of the system to the environment, or of the environment to the system." Wilden, *System and Structure*, 357.
16. "The open system is open to its environment, without which it cannot survive and on which it depends for those aspects of its . . . development which are not controlled by its internal rules and constraints." Wilden, *System and Structure*, 357.
17. Bertalanffy, *General Systems Theory*, 49.

18. Ervin Laszlo, *Introduction to Systems Philosophy: Toward a New Paradigm of Contemporary Thought* (New York: Gordon and Breach, 1972); Erich Jantsch, *Design for Evolution: Self-Organization and Planning in the Life of Human Systems* (New York: Braziller, 1975); Arthur Koestler, *The Act of Creation* (London: Hutchinson, 1964); Gregory Bateson, *Steps to an Ecology of Mind: Collected Essays in Anthropology, Psychiatry, Evolution, and Epistemology* (New York: Aronson, 1972).

19. See J. C. Smuts, *Holism and Evolution* (London: Macmillan, 1926). Smuts, a South African statesman and part-time philosopher, developed a theory of holism that gave an organicist account of everything from personality to the atom. Smuts advances an argument similar to that of Bertalanffy in that in wholes are manifest properties that are most contained as such in parts. However, Smuts is much more explicit about there being a transcendental character to the notion of holism. "We have seen that the creative intensified Field of Nature, consisting of all physical organic and personal wholes . . . is itself of an organic or wholistic character. That field is the source of the grand Ecology of the universe. It is the environment, the Society— vital, friendly, educative, creative— of all wholes and all souls" (p. 352). A similar organicist perspective contemporary to Smuts is A. N. Whitehead's doctrine of organic mechanism, which he developed in *Science and the Modern World* (Cambridge: Cambridge University Press, 1926), 99, 133–41.

20. Commoner, *The Closing Circle* (New York: Bantam Books, 1972).

21. A. G. Tansley, "The Use and Abuse of Vegetational Concepts and Terms," *Ecology* 16 (1935): 284–307.

22. See Wilden, *System and Structure*, xxxviii–ix.

23. See Robert Paehlke, *Environmentalism and the Future of Progressive Politics* (New Haven, Conn.: Yale University Press, 1989), 34–37.

24. Neil Evernden, *The Natural Alien: Humankind and Environment* (Toronto: University of Toronto Press, 1985), 18–25.

25. Ibid., 20.

26. Ibid., 33.

27. Writes Rozak: "Ecology has been called the 'subversive science'— and with good reason. Its sensibility—wholistic, receptive, trustful, largely non-tampering, deeply grounded in aesthetic tradition—is a

radical deviation from traditional science. Ecology does not system-
atize by mathematical generalization or materialist reduction, but by
the most sensuous intuiting of natural harmonies on the largest
scale. Its patterns are not those of numbers, but of unity in process;
its psychology borrows from Gestalt and is an awakening awareness
of wholes greater than the sum of their parts." T. Rozak, *Where the
Wasteland Ends* (Garden City, N.Y.: Doubleday, 1972), 400.

28. Murray Bookchin, *Post-Scarcity Anarchism* (Berkeley, Calif.:
Ramparts Press, 1971), 58.

29. Bradford, *How Deep is Deep Ecology?*, 3.

30. Donald Worster, *Nature's Economy: A History of Ecological Ideas*
(Cambridge: Cambridge University Press, 1977), 338.

31. Jean Baudrillard, "Modernity," *Canadian Journal of Political and
Social Theory* 113 (1987): 63–72.

32. Gianni Vattimo, *The End of Modernity: Nihilism and Hermeneutics in Postmodern Culture*, trans. Jon R. Snyder (Baltimore:
Johns Hopkins University Press, 1988), 6.

33. Mark C. Taylor, *Altarity* (Chicago: University of Chicago Press,
1987), xxii.

34. This early Frankfurt School work did reverberate somewhat into
social thinking about the environment and nature. Following
Horkheimer and Adorno, Herbert Marcuse developed further the
notion of enlightenment rationality and domination. Marcuse saw
in the counterculture movements of the 1960s and early 1970s the
beginnings of a kind of relationship with nature that was a fulfill-
ing of aesthetic needs. Such an expression or liberation of aesthetic
desire marked for Marcuse the revolutionary aspect of that time.
The disclosure and fulfillment of instinctual needs, in general, the
celebration of the pleasure principle, could act as a subversive force
with respect to the instrumental reason that characterizes modern
society. See Herbert Marcuse, *Eros and Civilization: A Philosophical Inquiry into Freud* (Boston: Beacon Press, 1974).

35. Max Horkheimer and Theodor Adorno, *The Dialectic of Enlightenment* (New York: Continuum, 1988), 9.

36. Ibid., 16.

37. "The pure immanence of positivism, its ultimate product, is no
more than a so to speak universal taboo. Nothing at all may
remain outside, because the mere idea of outsideness is the very
source of fear. The revenge of the primitive for death, when visited

upon one of his kin, was sometimes appeased by reception of the murderer into his own family; this, too, signified the infusion of alien blood into one's own, the generation of immanence." Ibid., 16.

38. Ibid., 7.
39. Ibid., xiv.
40. Ibid.
41. I refer here to a "successor science" not in the sense that Sandra Harding uses it (which I take to be an account of a science that is critically aware of its own artifice), but in the sense of a science that is more "true" and "natural." see Sandra Harding, *The Science Question in Feminism* (Ithaca, N.Y.: Cornell University Press, 1986).
42. Horkheimer and Adorno, *The Dialectic of Enlightenment*, 15.
43. Ibid., 12.
44. Tim Luke "The Dream of Deep Ecology," *Telos* 49 (Winter 1982): 77.
45. Michael Zimmerman, *Heidegger's Confrontation with Modernity: Technology, Politics, Art* (Bloomington: Indiana University Press, 1990), 8.
46. Paul Monaco, *Modern European Culture and Consciousness* (Albany: SUNY Press, 1983), 89–90.
47. Ibid., 91.
48. Jeffery Herf, *Reactionary Modernism: Technology, Culture and Politics in Weimar and the Third Reich* (Cambridge: Cambridge University Press, 1984).
49. Ibid., 1.
50. Jürgen Habermas, "Modernity—An Incomplete Project," *Anti-Aesthetic: Essays on Postmodern Culture*, ed. Hal Foster (San Francisco: Bay Press, 1983), 14.
51. Herf, *Reactionary Modernism*, 234.
52. Max Oelschlaeger, *The Idea of Wilderness: From Prehistory to the Age of Ecology* (New Haven, Conn.: Yale University Press, 1991), 302, 320. This very large work on the development of the idea of wilderness (paleolithic onward) will be the subject of a more detailed analysis below.
53. See Thomas Kuhn, *The Structure of Scientific Revolutions* (Chicago: University of Chicago Press, 1962), 10–42.
54. This of course completely bypasses the view of modernity and post-modernity as hinging on the very question (and possibility) of metanarratives. Cf. Lyotard's characterization of postmodernity as

an "incredulity towards metanarratives" Jean-François Lyotard, *The Postmodern Condition: A Report on Knowledge* (Minneapolis: University of Minnesota Press, 1984).

55. Thomas Kuhn, *The Essential Tension: Selected Studies in Scientific Tradition and Change* (Chicago: University of Chicago Press, 1977), 318–19.

56. George Grant, "Faith and the Multiversity," *Technology and Justice* (Toronto: Anansi Press, 1986), 36.

57. Alan Drengson, *Shifting Paradigms: From Technocrat to Planetary Person* (Victoria, B.C.: LightStar Press, 1983).

58. I refer here in passing to other philosophers and historians of science that have taken issue with Kuhn on a number of accounts. Cf. Paul Feyerabend, *Against Method* (London: Verso, 1975), *Science in a Free Society* (London: Verso, 1978), and I. Lakatos, and A. Musgrave, eds., *Criticism and the Growth of Knowledge* (Cambridge: Cambridge University Press, 1970).

59. See Drengson, *Shifting Paradigms*, 48–50. "We recognize that at several levels our society has undergone large scale changes over time. But it is not as if someone from two hundred years ago could not understand us, or we them" (p. 49).

60. Oelschlaeger, *The Idea of Wilderness*, 321.

61. Gianni Vattimo, "The End of (Hi)story," in *Zeitgeist in Babel: The Postmodernist Controversy* (Bloomington: Indiana University Press, 1991), 136.

62. Gianni Vattimo, *The End of Modernity* (Baltimore: Johns Hopkins University Press, 1988), 172.

63. Jean-François Lyotard, *Libidinal Economy* (Bloomington: Indiana University Press, 1993), 105.

64. In the extreme of Earth First!, the assumption seems to be that since civilization is acting out its biological ends in its relationship with the natural world, the only solution is to reject this intrinsic aspect and become other with nature. On some Earth First! accounts even this is not possible. Dave Foreman, one of the originators of Earth First! has described humanity as intrinsically a cancer on the Earth; on his account, one can read an interpretation of environmentalism that flatly rejects the place of humans in nature. For a recent interpretation of Earth First! as a millenarian/apocalyptic social movement, see Martha F. Lee, *Earth First!: Environmental Apocalypse* (Syracuse, N.Y.: Syracuse University Press, 1995).

3. Displacing the Humans

1. See Anthony Wilden, *System and Structure*, xxxvii–xliv. Wilden notes that apparent system theoretic holism (i.e., pseudoholism) on the order of the whole is more than the sum of the parts, and the implied projection of "system" and "environment" reveal on inspection either the familiar Cartesian schema of "subject" and "object," or the system itself "is viewed as an object, and moreover, an object to be viewed or even 'controlled' from an imaginary 'outside'" (p. xxxviii).
2. Mary Douglas, *Purity and Danger: An Analysis of the Concepts of Pollution and Taboo* (London: Arc Paperbacks, 1966), 7–28.
3. Evernden, *The Natural Alien*, 122.
4. Ibid., 117.
5. Fox, *Towards a Transpersonal Ecology*, 21–23.
6. I have intentionally not extended this idea to its obvious limit which would include the nonwhite, nonmale, and non-Euro-American. This level of critique (which is very much part of feminist theory) is not currently within the purview of radical environmentalism. See Trinh T. Minh-ha, *Woman, Native, Other: Writing Postcoloniality and Feminism* (Bloomington: Indiana University Press, 1989), 56, 94; Haraway, "The Promise of Monsters."
7. Haraway, "The Promise of Monsters," 311–13.
8. I use "orientalism" here in Edward Said's sense to denote the operation of hegemonic discourses about others—"Orientalism is a Western style for dominating, restructuring and having authority over the Orient. . . . Orientalism depends for its strategy on flexible positional superiority, which puts the Westerner in a whole series of possible relationships with the Orient without ever losing him the relative upper hand." *Orientalism* (New York, Vintage Books, 1978), 3–7. I am aware of the implication that Said's refiguring of the idea of orientalism may itself devolve into a reduction of the "West" into a seamless operation of discourse and power—an "Occidentalism," as Clifford calls it in *The Predicament of Culture*, 261. To the extent that it identifies a merging of ethnocentrism and monocentrism, orientalism need not be understood as an inversion. Of monocentrism, Said writes: "monocentrism is a concept I take in conjunction with ethnocentrism, the assumption that culture

masks itself as the sovereignty of *this* one and *this* human, whereas culture is the process of dominion and struggle always dissembling, always deceiving. Monocentrism is practiced when we mistake one idea as the only idea, instead of recognizing that an idea in history is always one among many. Monocentrism denies plurality, it totalizes structure, it sees profit where there is waste, it decrees the concentricity of Western culture instead of its excentricity." "The Text, the World, the Critic," *Textual Strategies: Perspectives in Post-Structural Criticism*, ed. Josué V. Harari (Ithaca, N.Y.: Cornell University Press, 1979), 161–88.

9. Bill Devall, *Simple in Means, Rich in Ends* (Salt Lake City, Utah: Gibbs Smith Publisher, 1988), 44–45.

10. Ibid., 39–40.

11. In his analysis of deep ecology, Tim Luke argues that the bio-eco-centric deep ecology position amounts to soft anthropocentrism: "an anthropocentrism that is more psychically rewarding or spiritually refreshing." It may well be that the deep ecologist feels a rewarding or gratifying sense of connection through the rhetoric of non-anthropocentrism, but the very fact of the subterfuge involved in the operation of ventriloquism makes me question the (too charitable) nature of Luke's claim. Tim Luke, "The Dream of Deep Ecology," *Telos* 49 (Winter 1982): 83.

12. See, for example, Christopher Manes, *Green Rage: Radical Environmentalism and the Unmaking of Civilization* (Boston: Little, Brown, 1990), 225–41.

13. To put this all quite differently, there is a desire to clean the baby off, and dump the bathwater of modernity. What deep ecology has failed to notice, is that the baby dissolved quite some time ago.

14. Deleuze and Guattari say of the secret: "The secret has a privileged, but quite variable relation to perception and the imperceptible. The secret relates first of all to certain contents. The content is *too* big for its form . . . or else the contents themselves have a form, but that form is covered, doubled, or replaced by a simple container, envelope, or box whose role is to suppress formal relations." *A Thousand Plateaus*, 288. To extend this notion of the secret, we could say that wilderness as a container of a secret becomes perceptible by virtue of its secretions. For instance, it may be disclosed publicly by those in on the secret—*wilderness is the place where real nature resides*. On the other hand, only the secretions are

disclosed, or the secretions are used to causally demonstrate the presence of the secret. This can take several forms. It may be a reading of impending disaster as a "message" issuing from nature, or it might be more explicitly moral reading of, for example, social disaster also as a message issuing from nature; in the extreme, AIDS as the revenge of the real. In any case, the wilderness secret may be used to tell a story either about the "proper" order of things, or it may be used to tell a different story about a natural retribution for having strayed from our *proper* course.

15. Clarence Glacken, *Traces on the Rhodian Shore: Nature and Culture in Western Thought from Ancient Times to the End of the Eighteenth Century* (Berkeley: University of California Press, 1967).

16. In an essay entitled "Wilderness, Civilization and Language," in *The Wilderness Condition: Essays on Environment and Civilization*, ed. Max Oelschlaeger (Washington D.C.: Island Press, 1992), Oelschlaeger claims that the reason wilderness literature is so often misunderstood as advocating a kind of primitivism is that the critics of this literature are unable to extract themselves from the modern, "Euro-language" heritage. He points to Anna Bramwell's book as a recent instance that the literature of wilderness is almost invariably misunderstood: "she clearly represents the modern mind at work: her worldview is that of Parmenides and Plato, of Descartes and Newton, of Locke and Adam Smith, of that human project which is Euro-culture. But language speaks, and those who equate the literature and rhetoric of the wilderness with primitivism thereby reveal the outlines of their own preconceptions of the world" (p. 272). The claim is thus that Bramwell "and her ilk" are unable to see beyond the binarity of the wilderness/culture configuration because of their rootedness in the language of the modern. Oelschlaeger's position seems to push in several directions simultaneously. In one sense he asserts a more or less paratheoretic insistence that any challenge (Bramwell's, or otherwise) must be founded upon a "modernist" linguistic worldview. And at the same time he advocates a move into a postmodern terrain in which the crisis of the modern is essentially linguistic. It is not a crisis of legitimation. It is not a crisis to be read in relation to the social and power. It senses that the crisis involves the referentiality of language, the arbitrary connection between linguistic signs (the so-

called linguistic turn), but seeks in response to rebuild a world linguistically. See Max Oelschlaeger, *Postmodern Environmental Ethics*, ed. Max Oelschlaeger (Albany, N.Y.: SUNY Press, 1995), 1–10. This odd sense of the postmodern speaks to this term's general ambiguity within contemporary theoretical and cultural discourses, and by implication, to a constant, and perhaps necessary confusion with respect to the meaning(s) of the modern.

17. The essay from which this well-used quote of Thoreau's is taken is entitled "Walking," *Harvard Classics*, Volume 28: *Essays English and American*, ed. Charles W. Elliot (New York: Collier Press, 1910), 407–38. It is partly a meditation on the virtues of the art of the saunter, and partly to do with his idea of the *west* as the place where wildness resides (*"ex oriente lux; ex Occidente FRUX*," p. 419). "The West of which I speak is but another name for the Wild. . . . Every tree sends its fibers forth in search of the Wild. The cities import it at any price. Men plough and sail for it. From the forest and wilderness come the tonics and barks that brace mankind. Our ancestors were savages" (p. 421).

18. Page numbers in parentheses indicate page references in the first edition of Max Oelschlaeger's *The Idea of Wilderness*.

19. He acknowledges that the following points are conjectural, but claims that nonetheless they are supported by "an array of anthropological and mythographical studies" (p. 11).

20. See Susan Bordo, "Feminism, Postmodernism and Gender-Skepticism," *Feminism/Postmodernism*, ed. Linda J. Nicholson (New York: Routledge, 1990).

21. Hans Duerr, *Dreamtime: Concerning the Boundary between Wilderness and Civilization* (Oxford: Basil Blackwell, 1985), 45, 109, 125.

22. Ibid., 125.

23. Ibid., 45. The final sentence of this quote is Duerr's own translation of a line from the *Dialectic of Enlightenment*.

24. Oelschlaeger, *The Idea of Wilderness*, 320–53. "And who are we but beings who have lost our animal innocence, grown ashamed of our nakedness and covered in garments of our own making, taking refuge in a dream world born from ideas that boil forth from our fevered imaginations. We, the spoiled children of the Great Mother, who refuse to see, to hear and heed Her message, Her laws. Is salvation possible?" (p. 353).

25. On this point, see also Michael Zimmerman, "The Blessing of Otherness," *The Wilderness Condition: Essays on Environment and Civilization*, 263–68. Note also that this essay appears to mark the point at which Zimmerman backs down from his previously enthusiastic embrace of Heidegger as a philosophical source of deep ecological inspiration. In addition to sources already cited, Zimmerman's Heideggerian deep ecology can be found in his *Heidegger's Confrontation with Modernity: Technology, Politics, Art* (Bloomington: Indiana University Press, 1990).
26. Duerr, *Dreamtime*, 133.
27. Trinh T. Minh-ha, *Woman, Native, Other*, 53–54.
28. Ibid., 76.
29. Ibid.
30. In addition to not wanting to become entangled in a debate about the American wilderness canon, I would also mention that, as a Canadian academic from a middle-class background, the summoning of the Thoreau, Muir, Leopold, Jeffers, Snyder "tradition" simply does not speak to a Canadian wilderness imaginary. My sense is that the Canadian wilderness draws its force from the image (Bordo) and from the landscape. Unlike the American wilderness, Canadian wilderness does not proceed from an "idea." For example, to have been born in Ontario is to know that Algonquin Park is—or depending on one's degree of involvement in such matters, was, but in either case, ought to be—wilderness. And having lived on the West Coast now for a period of time, I understand that here this imaginary operates in the register of Emily Carr; inside the trees are totems trying to get out. Canadian wilderness seems always subject to ostensive definition; the map and the image, and not the text. In "Jack Pine—wilderness sublime or the erasure of the aboriginal presence from the landscape, " Jonathan Bordo gives a provocative account of the manner in which Canadian wilderness has been constituted by the humanless landscape traditions exemplified by the Group of Seven. On his account, wilderness as a pictorial representation has come to be replaced, through a mimetic reversal, by the empty wilderness precinct—that is, park. The key point being that wilderness begins as a denial of the human form in landscape representations, subsequently becomes fixed into cultural practices—a cultural ethos, he says—concerning wilderness, which then results in the constitution of wilderness as an empty place. The

circle completes itself at the point which the wilderness precinct comes to draw its support from the very images which founded it to begin with. See also, Jonathan Bordo, "The Witness in the Errings of Contemporary Art," *The Rhetoric of the Frame*, ed. Paul Duro (Cambridge: Cambridge University Press, 1996), 278–302. For another account of the relationships between the painted landscape and the materiality of Canadian wilderness, see Scott Watson, "Race, Wilderness, Territory and the Origins of Modern Canadian Landscape Painting," *Semiotext(e) Canadas*, ed. Jordan Zinovich (New York: Semiotext(e), 1994), 93–104.

31. Clastres, *Society against the State*, 202.

32. Ibid., 211–12. Clastres's work is based on an extensive working knowledge of South and North American aboriginal cultures. It is obviously beyond the scope of this work to evaluate the fieldwork which supports his political ethnography. It is also beyond the scope of this work to engage the apparent paradox that Clastres's work raises. This paradox, brought to light by Deleuze and Guattari, consists in how primitive social organization can be structured around a prohibition for that which does not exist—that is, coercive power and its embodiment in the form of a State. "In the final state of his work, Clastres maintained the preexistence and autarky of counter-State societies, and attributed their workings to an over mysterious presentiment of what they warded off and did not yet exist." See Deleuze and Guattari, *A Thousand Plateaus*, 357–99, 429.

33. Devall and Sessions, *Deep Ecology*, 96. Most texts concerned with deep ecology that touch on the category "primitive" make explicit reference to a distinction between a deep ecological conception of the primitive and to other less sophisticated representations. Cf. Devall, *Simple in Means, Rich in Ends*, 199–201; Oelschlaeger, *The Idea of Wilderness*, 110–13; Manes, *Green Rage*, 237–41.

34. On this point, see Mick Smith, "Cheney and the Myth of Postmodernism," *The Wilderness Condition*, 261–76.

35. Shepard sees evidence of repressed wildness in, for example, the increasing popularity of organic meat and daily exercise, in the contested status of sport-hunting, in the cult of the vegetable (i.e., vegetarians), and in the naming of domestic pets. Paul Shepard, "A Post-Historic Primitivism," *The Wilderness Condition*, 40–89. See also Paul Shepard, *Nature and Madness* (San Francisco: Sierra Club Books, 1982).

36. Shepard, "A Post-Historic Primitivism," 79.
37. Marianna Torgovnick, *Gone Primitive: Savage Intellects, Modern Lives* (Chicago: University of Chicago Press, 1990), 9.
38. See Wilden, *System and Structure*, 155–90.
39. Elizabeth Grosz, *Jacques Lacan: A Feminist Introduction* (New York: Routledge, 1990), 202n5.
40. Torgovnick, *Gone Primitive*, 9.
41. "Freud's map of the psyche placed the ego (the Ich, the I) at a point that mediates between the civilized super-ego and the 'primitive' libido (or id). Whether this map was accurate or not is less important that its strength as a metaphor for our time. We conceive of ourselves as at a crossroads between the civilized and the savage; we are formed by our conceptions of both those terms, conceived dialectically." Torgovnick, *Gone Primitive*, 17.
42. The production of twenty-four Tarzan novels and over fifty movies fed an ever-increasing Western appetite for tales from the Dark Continent. Interestingly though, Torgovnick sees in Burroughs an attempt to challenge the construction of ethnographic categories. See Torgovnick, *Gone Primitive*, 42–72.
43. William S. Burroughs, "Thanksgiving Day, Nov. 28, 1986," *Tornado Alley* (Ann Arbor, Mich.: Cherry Valley Editions, 1989), 7.
44. Torgovnick, *Gone Primitive*, 188.
45. Ibid., 13.
46. Ibid., 17.
47. Ibid., 20.
48. Ibid., 245.
49. Jonathan Bordo, "The Solitary Jack Pine: Becoming Tree or the Erasure of the Aboriginal Presence from the Visual Image of the Land," unpublished ms (Peterborough: Trent University, 1990), 32. This argument receives a slightly altered but more complete treatment in "Jack Pine—Wilderness Sublime or the Erasure of the Aboriginal Presence from the Landscape," *Journal of Canadian Studies*, 27.4 (1992): 98–128.
50. To which he adds, "[F]rom it [the Kantian wilderness formulation] emerges the following maxim for action: Leave no traces behind." "Jack Pine Wilderness Sublime or the Erasure of the Aboriginal Presence from the Landscape," 121.
51. See Note 30 above.

4. Boundary Disputes

1. A useful note on terminology. Elizabeth Grosz has pointed out an interesting taxonomy or classification of terms which are often conflated under the term essentialism ("A Note on Essentialism and Difference," *Feminist Knowledge: Critique and Construct*, ed. Sneja Gunew (New York: Routledge, 1990), 332–44). Essentialism, she notes, is a term that needs to be disentangled from its cognates *biologism*, *naturalism*, and *universalism*. Essentialism refers to the existence of fixed characteristics and attributes (not necessarily biological, that is, the nurturing and empathy of women, naturalness of the primitive, authenticity of wilderness), and ahistorical functions that limit the possibility of change. Biologism is a form of essentialism that posits social difference in terms of biological causes; if biology is assumed to be the ground of identity, biologism also accounts for constraints upon change and the possibilities of resistance. Naturalism (also a form of essentialism), while most often asserted on grounds of biology, may also be asserted on ontological or theoretical grounds. Proximate to these three is universalism, which, also justified on biological or natural grounds, may also be given as socially specified. Thus, for example, Evernden's account of humans as misfits (discussed above) would be an example of a form of biologism. But since it is also an encompassing term, it has a sense of universalism. Yet, in addition to this, because it is fundamentally an ontological function (neotony), it is also a form of naturalism.
2. See Rosi Braidotti, *Nomadic Subjects* (New York: Routledge, 1994), 57–60.
3. Haraway, *Simians, Cyborgs and Women: The Reinvention of Nature* (New York: Routledge, 1991), 151–52. And parenthetically, she adds, "Within this framework, teaching modern Christian creationism should be fought as a form of child abuse."
4. See also Haraway's *Primate Visions: Gender, Race and Nature in the World of Modern Science* (New York: Routledge, 1989). In this extraordinary work she engages the field of primate studies and science as a lively battlefield in the outer ramparts of the category "human." This particular boundary dispute about humans and primates reverberates throughout academic, intellectual, and social spheres: "between psychiatry and zoology, biology and anthro-

pology, genetics and comparative psychology, ecology and medical research, agriculturalist and tourist industries in the 'third world,' field researchers and laboratory scientists, conservationist and multinational logging companies, poacher and game wardens, scientists and administrators of zoos, feminists and antifeminists, specialists and lay people, physical anthropologist and ecological-evolutionary biologists, established scientists and new Ph.D.'s, women's studies students and professors in animal behavior courses, linguists and biologists, foundation officials and grant applications, science writers and researchers, historians of science and real scientists, marxists and liberals, liberals and neo-conservatives" (p. 14).

5. Haraway, *Simians, Cyborgs and Women*, 147.

6. Ibid., 152.

7. Ibid.

8. Jean Baudrillard, *Xerox and Infinity* (London: Touchepas, 1988), not paginated. Reprinted and retranslated in Jean Baudrillard, *The Transparency of Evil: Essays on Extreme Phenomena* (London: Verso, 1993), 51–59.

9. Georges Canguilhem, "Machine and Organism," *Zone 6: Incorporations*, ed. Jonathan Crary and Sanford Kwinter, trans. Mark Cohen and Randal Cherry (New York: Zone, 1992), 45–69. Canguilhem considers what he sees to be the historical reversal of the traditional (Cartesian) relationship between the machine and the organism. "The relationship between the machine and organism has been studied in only one way. Nearly always the organism has been explained on the basis of a preconceived idea of the structure and functioning of the machine; but only rarely have the structure and functioning of the organism been used to make the construction of the machine itself more understandable. Even though mechanistic theory sparked some very impressive technical results, the fact remained that the very notion of an "organology," as well as its basic premises and methodology, remained undeveloped" (p. 45).

10. William Gibson, *Neuromancer* (New York: Ace, 1984).

11. Peter Fitting, "The Lessons of Cyberpunk," *Technoculture*, ed. Constance Penley and Andrew Ross (Minneapolis: University of Minnesota Press, 1991), 295–315. I would take issue with his qualifying the relations of technology and the human as based on a dependency to re-present. From my reading of Gibson, I would say

that the relationship is not nuanced by a dependency, but is so diffused as to be understood as a *dwelling within.*

12. Ibid., 305.
13. One could at this point read a convergence or resonance between
    this idea and certain notions of bioregional involvement.
14. Haraway, *Simians, Cyborgs and Women*, 149.
15. Ibid., 151.
16. Ibid., 151.
17. Ibid., 154.
18. Ibid., 181.
19. Teresa de Lauretis, ed., *Feminist Studies/Critical Studies* (Blooming-
    ton: Indiana University Press, 1986), 9.
20. Haraway, *Simians, Cyborgs and Women*, 187. "History is a story
    Western culture buffs tell each other; science is a contestable text
    and a power field; the content is the form. Period." (p. 185).
21. Haraway, "Cyborgs at Large: Interview with Donna Haraway,"
    Technoculture, 2.
22. Haraway, *Simians, Cyborgs and Women*, 187.
23. Ibid., 187.
24. Martin Heidegger, "The Question Concerning Technology,"
    Martin Heidegger: Basic Writings, ed. David Farrell Krell (New
    York: Harper & Row, 1977), 310–17.
25. Gibson is often credited with having invented the aesthetic of
    cyberpunk (P. K. Dick notwithstanding). It took not long for that
    aesthetic, or at least a West Coast simulacrum, to be reworked as a
    techno-hedonistic array of commodities. A good example is to be
    found in the emergence of the virtual reality and cyberpunk advo-
    cate *Mondo 2000* (previously *Reality Hackers*). This hightech
    bimonthly out of Berkeley, California, is a self-proclaimed leader in
    "New Edge" matters. "Mondo 2000 will introduce you to your
    tomorrow—and show you how to buy it today!" Its patron saint:
    McLuhan. The promise of technology to liberate humans (at least
    those humans with sufficient income) from the constraints of the
    body is the ground of the *Mondo* New Edge; a pharmacopoeia of
    smart drugs to increase intelligence and memory, virtual reality
    software to (re)create in user-defined virtual spaces, DMT and rave
    culture, and cyberpunk as a style within which to negotiate new
    edge culture. Although this can all seem annoyingly white, middle
    class, and particularly a-political in its liberal solipsism, it is

nonetheless a fascinating document. See also Mondo's compendium to the new edge: Rudy Rucker, and R. U. Sirius, eds., *Mondo 2000: A User's Guide to the New Edge* (New York: HarperCollins, 1992). All of the cyber-constituency addressed by *Mondo 2000*, together with a new-edge alphabet including neopagans, cyber disco, hackers, and answers to such questions as Why is this music always pounding at 120 beats per minute?, is discussed in Douglas Rushkoff, *Cyberia: Life in the Trenches of Hyperspace* (San Francisco: HarperCollins, 1994). While I don't recommend this particular volume for its interpretive scope, it is a great vicarious tour through "cyberia."

26. Bilateral symmetry seems to mark the imaginative limit in this particular fictive rendering of others.
27. Haraway, "The Promise of Monsters," 300, 333n18.
28. Ibid., 297.
29. Ibid., 289.
30. Ibid., 297.
31. Ibid.
32. Bruno Latour, "An Interview with Bruno Latour," *Configurations* 2 (1993): 282. A sense of where Latour is positioned in this murky zone of modernity/postmodernity is given in the following: "The modern view divides the constitution between the representation of humans and the representation of nonhumans and also creates the difference between 'us' and 'them' in culture. All the other cultures don't make this distinction; we do. There is a complete similarity between the internal divide between the representation of human and of nonhuman and the external great divide between the cultures. Now this modern regime, this whole arrangement, is coming to a close when you cross the two denunciations, and that is where the postmodern definition comes in. I call postmodernism the 'disappointed' version of these two: it is a disappointed enlightenment plus a disappointed critique coming from the social sciences. It still wants to criticize, but it doesn't have the ground to criticize because it doesn't believe any more in the promises of socialism or of naturalism. That is why postmodernism is an interesting symptom and a complete failure intellectually (although this might not be the case for the arts). Post-modern thinkers have absolutely no idea how they can go on doing criticism without having a foundation. So then the question is can we play another game? Can we redefine

the task of the intellectual so that it is no longer denouncing from one of two poles? That is what I call 'nonmodernism' (the name is terrible and it should disappear soon). The nonmodernist argument is the realization that we have never been modern in the first place, so it is not a new revolution, like postmodernism coming after modernism. Suddenly we realize that a supermarket, a laboratory, and a machine are not made from ingredients radically different from the past; they only have slight differences which have to be empirically recovered. Of course, when viewed from a post-modernist point this is totally reactionary, but it is not antimodern. It is simply not modern (in the sense I have given) because it does not make the distinction between the representation of humans and the representation of nonhumans—hence its similarity and fraternity with the so-called premoderns, the famous Others to whom We were supposed to be radically opposed. Now we know that there is no such thing as the representation of the human and the representation of the nonhuman; they are mixed in whichever subject you take" (pp. 281–82).

33. Haraway, "The Promise of Monsters," 330n6.
34. Ibid.
35. Bruno Latour, *We Have Never Been Modern* (Cambridge, Mass.: Harvard University Press, 1993), 134.
36. Deleuze and Parnet, *Dialogues*, 52. See also pp. vii–x.
37. Ibid.
38. Haraway, *Simians, Cyborgs and Women*, 181.
39. Ibid., 191.
40. Ibid., 193. And, we may add, in environmental literature, as the essentialized aboriginal person.
41. Ibid.
42. Rosi Braidotti, "Toward a New Nomadism," unpublished ms (Holland: University of Utrecht, 1991), 22.
43. Ibid., 196ff.
44. Alphonso Lingis, *The Community of Those Who Have Nothing in Common* (Baltimore: Johns Hopkins University Press, 1994), 87–88.
45. Christina Crosby, "Allies and Enemies," *Coming to Terms: Feminism, Theory, Politics*, ed. Elizabeth Weed (New York: Routledge, 1989), 207.
46. Ibid., 208.

47. See Giorgio Agamben, *The Coming Community* (Minneapolis: University of Minnesota Press, 1993); cf. sections entitled "The Irreparable," and "Ethics."
48. Braidotti, "Toward a New Nomadism," 22.
49. Blanchot, *The Writing of the Disaster* (Lincoln: University of Nebraska Press, 1986), 18.
50. Lingis, *The Community of Those Who Have Nothing in Common*, 25.
51. Ibid., 20.
52. Ibid., 26.
53. It strikes me that there is a relationship between what Deleuze would call an *a priori* Other, or structure-other, and what Lingis here describes as forms of an ordering process. Deleuze describes the *a priori* Other not as an alternative between an object in a perceptual field, or a subject of that field, but as a preexisting structure within which the actualization of others takes place. This structure is the structure of the possible, and hence the other—when actualized within a perceptual field—is the *expression* of a possible world. The surface-sensitivity is an acknowledgment of a concrete Other— an other subject that I actualize as a possible world—insofar as I am the actualization of a possible world *for that other subject*. Depth perception as I understand it would seem to strip the other of its quality of being a possible world by forcing it to conform to another structure. In other words, the other-in-depth-perception is disavowed as a possible world, and actualized only insofar as it attaches to terms in a world which preexists. See Deleuze's analysis of Tournier's novel, *Friday*, in Gilles Deleuze, *The Logic of Sense* (New York: Columbia University Press, 1990), 301–21.
54. Here I refer implicitly to the work that follows and develops Freud's, "The Dynamics of the Transference (1912)," *Collected Papers*, volume 2, trans. Joan Riviere (New York: Basic Books, 1959), 312–22. Writers such as George Dévereux, *From Anxiety to Method in the Behavioral Sciences* (The Hague: Mouton, 1968), and J. Laplanche and J.-B. Pontalis, *The Language of Psychoanalysis* (New York: Norton, 1973) could be of great value to the project of understanding the manner in which the problematic of the Other cannot be settled by appeal to the primitive.
55. Iain Chambers, *Border Dialogues: Journeys in Postmodernity* (New York: Routledge, 1990), 94.

56. Ibid., 95.
57. Ibid.
58. Ibid.
59. See Gary Genosko, "The Struggle for Affirmative Weakness: de Certeau, Lyotard, and Baudrillard," *Current Perspectives in Social Theory* 12 (1992): 179–94. This essay is given in revised form in a larger treatment of Baudrillard's semiological games in his *Baudrillard and Signs: Signification Ablaze* (New York: Routledge, 1994), 72–81.
60. Giovanna Borradori, "'Weak Thought' and Postmodernism: The Italian Departure from Deconstruction," *Social Text* 18 (1988): 39.
61. Ibid., 40.
62. Chambers, *Border Dialogues*, 96. See also Genosko, *Baudrillard and Signs*, 72–3.
63. Borradori, "'Weak Thought' and Postmodernism," 44.
64. Vattimo, "The End of (Hi)story," 136–37.
65. *The End of Modernity*, xxvi; see also pp. 172, 175–76, and Vattimo, *The Transparent Society* (Baltimore: Johns Hopkins University Press, 1992), 41–43.
66. Vattimo, "The End of (Hi)story," 139.
67. Gianni Vattimo and Pier Aldo Rovatti eds., Foreword in *Il pensiero debole* (Milan: Feltrinelli, 1983), quoted (and translated) in Giovanna Borradori, "'Weak Thought' and Postmodernism," 43.
68. Mary Ann Doane, "Cyborgs, Origins and Subjectivities," *Coming to Terms: Feminism, Theory, Politics*, ed. Elizabeth Weed (New York: Routledge, 1989), 212–13.
69. Ibid., 213.
70. Ibid., 213–14 (italics mine).
71. I refer to Derrida's essay on Lévi-Strauss, "Structure, Sign and Play in the Discourse of the Human Sciences," *Writing and Difference*, trans. Alan Bass (Chicago: University of Chicago Press, 1978), 278–93.
72. Ibid., 280.
73. Ibid., 284.
74. Michel Foucault, "Intellectuals and Power: A Conversation between Michel Foucault and Gilles Deleuze," *Language, Counter-memory, Practice: Selected Essays and Interviews*, ed. Donald Bouchard, trans. Donald F. Bouchard and Sherry Smith (Ithaca, N.Y.: Cornell University Press, 1977), 208.

75. Ibid. Deleuze continues, "It has nothing to do with the signifier. It must be useful. It must function. And not for itself. If no one uses it, beginning with the theoretician (who then ceases to be a theoretician), then the theory is worthless, or the moment inappropriate. We don't revise a theory, but construct new ones; we have no choice but to make others. It is strange that it was Proust, an author thought to be a pure intellectual, who said it so clearly: treat my book as a pair of glasses directed to the outside; if they don't suit you, find another pair; I leave it to you to find your own instrument, which is necessarily an instrument for combat."

Bibliography

Austin, Richard Cartwright. "Beauty: A Foundation for Environmental Ethics." *Environmental Ethics* 7 (1985): 197–208.

Bateson, Gregory. *Mind and Nature: A Necessary Unity.* New York: E. P. Dutton, 1979.

———. *Steps to an Ecology of Mind: Collected Essays in Anthropology, Psychiatry, Evolution, and Epistemology.* New York: Aronson, 1972.

Baudrillard, Jean. *The Mirror of Production.* Translated by Mark Poster. New York: Telos, 1975.

———. "Modernity." *Canadian Journal of Political and Social Theory* 113 (1987): 63–72.

———. *The Transparency of Evil: Essays on Extreme Phenomena.* Translated by James Benedict. London: Verso, 1993.

———. *Xerox and Infinity.* Translated by Agitac. New York: Touchepas, 1988.

Benjamin, Walter. *Illuminations: Essays and Reflections.* Translated by Harry Zohn. New York: Schocken Books, 1968.

Birch, Thomas. "The Incarceration of Wildness: Wilderness Areas as Prisons." *Environmental Ethics* 12 (1990): 3–26.

Blumenberg, Hans. *The Genesis of the Copernican World.* Cambridge, Mass.: MIT Press, 1987.

Bookchin, Murray. *Ecology and Revolutionary Thought.* New York: Times Change Press, 1970.

———. *The Philosophy of Social Ecology: Essays on Dialectical Naturalism.* Montreal: Black Rose Books, 1990.

————. *Post-Scarcity Anarchism*. New York: Rampart Press, 1971.

————. *Remaking Society*. Montreal: Black Rose Books, 1989.

————. *Toward an Ecological Society*. Montreal: Black Rose Books, 1980.

Bookchin, Murray, and David Foreman. *Defending the Earth*. Montreal: Black Rose Books, 1991.

Bookchin, Murray, Graham Purchase, Brian Morris, and Rodney Aitchtey. *Deep Ecology and Anarchism: A Polemic*. London: Freedom Press, 1993.

Bordo, Jonathan. "Ecological Peril, Modern Technology and the Postmodern Sublime." In *Shadow of Spirit: Postmodernism and Religion*. Edited by P. Berry and Andrew Wernick. New York: Routledge, 1993, pp. 165–78.

————. "Jack Pine—Wilderness Sublime or the Erasure of the Aboriginal Presence from the Landscape." *Journal of Canadian Studies* 27.4 (1992): 98–128.

————. "The Witness in the Errings of Contemporary Art." In *The Rhetoric of the Frame*. Edited by Paul Duro. Cambridge: Cambridge University Press, 1996, pp. 278–302.

Bordo, Susan. "Feminism, Postmodernism and Gender-Skepticism." In *Feminism/Postmodernism*. Edited by Linda J. Nicholson. New York: Routledge, 1990.

Borradori, Giovanna. "'Weak Thought' and Postmodernism: The Italian Departure from Deconstruction." *Social Text* 18 (1988): 39–49.

Bradford, George. *How Deep is Deep Ecology?* New York: Times Change Press, 1989.

Braidotti, Rosi. *Nomadic Subjects*. New York: Routledge, 1994.

————. *Patterns of Dissonance: A Study of Women in Contemporary Philosophy*. Translated by Elizabeth Guild. New York: Routledge, 1991.

————. "Toward a New Nomadism," unpublished ms. Holland: University of Utrecht, 1991.

Bramwell, Anna. *Ecology in the 20th Century: A History*. New Haven, Conn.: Yale University Press, 1989.

Bukatman, Scott. *Terminal Identity: The Virtual Subject in Postmodern Science Fiction*. Raleigh, N.C.: Duke University Press, 1993.

Burroughs, William S. "Thanksgiving Day, Nov. 28, 1986." *Tornado Alley*. Ann Arbor, Mich.: Cherry Valley Editions, 1989.

Butler, Judith. *Gender Trouble: Feminism and the Subversion of Identity.* New York: Routledge, 1990.

Bynum, W., E. Browne, and R. Porter, eds. *Dictionary of the History of Science.* Princeton, N.J.: Princeton University Press, 1981.

Canguilhem, Georges. "Machine and Organism." In *Zone 6: Incorporations.* Edited by Jonathan Crary and Sanford Kwinter. Translated by Mark Cohen and Randal Cherry. New York: Zone, 1992, pp. 45–69.

Capra, F. *Tao of Physics: Science, Society, and the Rising Culture.* New York: Flamingo, 1976.

———.*Turning Point: Science, Society and the Rising Culture.* New York: Bantam Books, 1983.

Carson, Rachel. *Silent Spring.* Boston: Houghton Mifflin, 1962.

Chambers, Iain. *Border Dialogues: Journeys in Postmodernity.* New York: Routledge, 1990.

Cheney, Jim. "Eco-Feminism and Deep Ecology." *Environmental Ethics* 9 (1987): 115–45.

Clastres, Pierre. *Archaeology of Violence.* Translated by Jeanine Herman. New York: Semiotext(e), 1994.

———. *Society against the State: Essays in Political Anthropology.* Translated by Robert Hurley. New York: Zone Books, 1987.

Clifford, James. "Fieldwork, Reciprocity and the Making of Ethnographic Texts." *Man* 153 (1980): 518–32.

———. *The Predicament of Culture: Twentieth-Century Ethnography, Literature, and Art.* Cambridge, Mass.: Harvard University Press, 1988.

Commoner, Barry. *The Closing Circle.* New York: Bantam Books, 1972.

DeLanda, Manuel. "Nonorganic Life." In *Zone 6: Incorporations.* Edited by Jonathan Crary and Sanford Kwinter. New York: Zone Books, 1992, pp. 129–67.

Deleuze, Gilles. *Negotiations, 1972–1990.* Translated by Mark Joughin. New York: Columbia University Press, 1995.

———. *Nietzsche and Philosophy.* Translated by Hugh Tomlinson. New York: Columbia University Press, 1983.

Deleuze, Gilles, and Félix Guattari. *Kafka: Toward a Minor Literature.* Translated by Dana Polan. Minneapolis: University of Minnesota Press, 1986.

———. *A Thousand Plateaus.* Translated by Brian Massumi. Minneapolis: University of Minnesota Press, 1987.

Deleuze, Gilles, and Claire Parnet. *Dialogues*. Translated by Hugh Tomlinson and Barbara Habberjam. New York: Columbia University Press, 1977.

Derrida, Jacques. "Structure, Sign and Play in the Discourse of the Human Sciences." *Writing and Difference*. Translated by Alan Bass. Chicago: University of Chicago Press, 1978, pp. 278–293.

Devall, Bill. "The Deep Ecology Movement." *Natural Resources Journal* 20 (1980): 299–322.

———. *Simple in Means, Rich in Ends: Practicing Deep Ecology*. New York: Gibbs Smith, 1988.

Devall, Bill, and George Sessions. *Deep Ecology: Living as if Nature Mattered*. Salt Lake City, Utah: Peregrine Books, 1985.

Dévereux, George. *From Anxiety to Method in the Behavioral Sciences*. The Hague: Mouton, 1986.

diZerega, Gus. "Empathy, Society, Nature, and the Relational Self: Deep Ecology and Liberal Modernity." *Social Theory and Practice* 21.2 (1995): 239–69.

———. "Social Ecology, Deep Ecology, and Liberalism." *Critical Review* 6.2–3 (1992): 305–70.

Doane, Mary Ann. "Cyborgs, Origins and Subjectivities." In *Coming to Terms: Feminism, Theory, Politics*. Edited by Elizabeth Weed. New York: Routledge, 1989.

Dobson, Andrew. "Deep Ecology." *Cogito* 3.1 (1989): 41–46.

Douglas, Mary. *Purity and Danger: An Analysis of the Concepts of Pollution and Taboo*. London: Arc, 1966.

Drengson, Alan. "A Critique of Deep Ecology? Response to William Grey." *Journal of Applied Philosophy* 4 (1987): 223–27.

———. *Shifting Paradigms: From Technocrat to Planetary Person*. Victoria, B.C.: LightStar Press, 1983.

Drengson, Alan, and Yuichi Inoue, eds. *The Deep Ecology Movement: An Introductory Anthology*. Berkeley, Calif.: North Atlantic Books, 1995.

Dreyfus, Hubert L., and Paul Rabinow. *Michel Foucault: Beyond Structuralism and Hermeneutics*. Chicago: University of Chicago Press, 1983.

Duerr, Hans Peter. *Dreamtime: Concerning the Boundary between Wilderness and Civilization*. Translated by Felicitas Goodman. Oxford: Basil Blackwell, 1985.

Eckersley, Robyn. *Environmentalism and Political Theory: Toward and Ecocentric Approach.* Albany, N.Y.: SUNY Press, 1992.

Eliade, M. *The Sacred and the Profane.* New York: HBJ Books, 1959.

Emery, F. *Systems Thinking,* vol. 2. New York: Penguin, 1981.

Environmental Action, ed. *Earth Day—The Beginning.* New York: Bantam, 1970.

Evernden, Neil. *The Natural Alien: Humankind and Environment.* Toronto: University of Toronto Press, 1985.

———, ed. *The Paradox of Environmentalism.* North York, York University: Faculty of Environmental Studies, 1984.

Ewald, François. "Two Infinities of Risk." *The Politics of Everyday Fear.* Translated by Brian Massumi. Minneapolis: University of Minnesota Press, 1993, pp. 221–28.

Feyerabend, Paul. *Against Method: Outline of an Anarchistic Theory of Knowledge.* London: Verso, 1984.

———. *Science in a Free Society.* London: Verso, 1982.

Finlay, Marike. "Rethinking the Subject in Discourse: From Relative Subjectivities to the Ontology of Subject as Related Interiority." *Discours social / Social Discourse* 2.1–2 (1989): ix–liii.

Fitting, Peter. "The Lessons of Cyberpunk." *Technoculture.* Edited by Constance Penley and Andrew Ross. Minneapolis: University of Minnesota Press, 1991, pp. 295–315.

Foreman, David. *Ecodefense: A Field Guide to Monkeywrenching.* Tuscon, Ariz.: Nedd Ludd Books, 1991.

Foster, Hal. "The Primitive Unconscious of Modern Art." *October* 34 (1985): 45–70.

Foucault, Michel. *Discipline and Punish: The Birth of the Prison.* Translated by Alan Sheridan. New York: Vintage Books, 1979.

———."Intellectuals and Power: A Conversation between Michel Foucault and Gilles Deleuze." In *Language, Counter-memory, Practice: Selected Essays and Interviews.* Edited by Donald Bouchard. Translated by Donald F. Bouchard and Sherry Smith. Ithaca, N.Y.: Cornell University Press, 1977, pp. 205–17.

———. "Nietzsche, Marx, Freud." In *Transforming the Hermeneutic Context: From Nietzsche to Nancy.* Edited by G. Ormiston and A. Schrift. Albany, N.Y.: SUNY Press, 1990, pp. 59–67.

Fox, Warwick. "The Deep Ecology-Ecofeminism Debate and Its Parallels." *Environmental Ethics* 11 (1989): 5–25.

———. "Deep Ecology: A New Philosophy for our Time?" *Ecologist* 14 (1984): 194–200.

———. *Toward a Transpersonal Ecology: Developing New Foundations for Environmentalism.* Boston: Shambhala, 1990.

French, William C. "Against Biospherical Egalitarianism." *Environmental Ethics* 17 (1995): 39–57.

Freud, Sigmund. "The Dynamics of the Transference (1912)." *Collected Papers*, vol. 2. Translated by Joan Riviere. New York: Basic Books, 1959, pp. 312–22.

Genosko, Gary. "The Struggle for Affirmative Weakness: de Certeau, Lyotard, and Baudrillard." *Current Perspectives in Social Theory* 12 (1992): 179–94.

Gibson, William. *Neuromancer.* New York: Ace, 1984.

Glacken, Clarence. *Traces on the Rhodian Shore: Nature and Culture in Western Thought from Ancient Times to the End of the Eighteenth Century.* Berkeley: University of California Press, 1973.

Gleick, James. *Chaos: Making a New Science.* New York: Penguin, 1987.

Golley, Frank B. "Deep Ecology from the Perspective of Environmental Science." *Environmental Ethics* 9 (1987): 45–55.

Goulding, J. *Empire, Aliens and Conquest: A Critique of American Ideology in Star Trek and other Science Fiction Adventures.* Toronto: Sisyphus Press, 1985.

Grant, George. *Technology and Empire.* Toronto: Anansi, 1969.

Greenblatt, Stephen. *Marvelous Possessions: The Wonder of the New World.* Chicago: University of Chicago Press, 1991.

Grey, William. "Anthropocentrism and Deep Ecology." *Australasian Journal of Philosophy* 71 (1993): 463–75.

———. "A Critique of Deep Ecology." *Journal of Applied Philosophy* 3.2 (1986): 211–16.

Grosz, Elizabeth. *Jacques Lacan: A Feminist Introduction.* New York: Routledge, 1990.

———. "A Note on Essentialism and Difference." In *Feminist Knowledge: Critique and Construct.* Edited by Sneja Gunew. New York: Routledge, 1990, pp. 332–44.

Grumbine, Edward R. "Wildness, Wise Use, and Sustainable Development." *Environmental Ethics* 16 (1994): 227–49.

Guattari, Félix. "The Three Ecologies." *New Formations* 8 (1989): 131–47.

Guha, Ramachandra. "Radical American Environmentalism and Wilderness Preservation: A Third World Critique." *Environmental Ethics* 11 (1989): 71–83.

Habermas, Jürgen. "Modernity—An Incomplete Project." In *Anti-Aesthetic: Essays on Postmodern Culture*. Edited by Hal Foster. San Francisco: Bay Press, 1983, pp. 3–15.

Haraway, Donna. "The Actors are Cyborgs, Nature is Coyote, and the Geography is Elsewhere: Postscript to 'Cyborgs at Large'." In *Technoculture*. Edited by Constance Penley and Andrew Ross. Minneapolis: University of Minnesota Press, 1991, pp. 21–26.

———. "Cyborgs at Large: Interview with Donna Haraway." In *Technoculture*. Edited by Constance Penley and Andrew Ross. Minneapolis: University of Minnesota Press, 1991, pp. 1–20.

———. "Ecce Homo, Ain't (Ar'n't) I a Woman, and Inappropriate/d Others: The Human in a Post-Humanist Landscape." In *Feminists Theorize the Political*. Edited by Judith Butler and Joan Scott. New York: Routledge, 1992, pp. 86–100.

———. "The Promise of Monsters: A Regenerative Politics for Inappropriate/d Others." In *Cultural Studies*. Edited by L. Grossberg, C. Nelson, and P. Treichler. New York: Routledge, 1992, pp. 295–337.

———. *Simians, Cyborgs and Women: The Reinvention of Nature*. New York: Routledge, 1991.

———. "When Man™ is on the Menu." In *Zone 6: Incorporations*. Edited by Jonathan Crary and Sanford Kwinter. New York: Zone, 1992, pp. 39–43.

Hardin, Garrett. "The Tragedy of the Commons." In *Economics, Ecology, Ethics: Essays towards a Steady State Economy*. Edited by Herman Daly. New York: Freeman, 1985, pp. 100–114.

Harding, Sandra. *The Science Question in Feminism*. Ithaca, N.Y.: Cornell University Press, 1986.

Heidegger, Martin. *Martin Heidegger: Basic Writings*. Edited by David Farrell Krell. New York: Harper & Row, 1977.

Herf, Jeffery. *Reactionary Modernism: Technology, Culture and Politics in Weimar and the Third Reich*. Cambridge: Cambridge University Press, 1984.

Horkheimer, Max, and Theodor Adorno. *The Dialectic of Enlightenment*. Translated by John Cummings. New York: Continuum, 1988.

Huizinga, Johan. *Homo Ludens: A Study of the Play Element in Culture*. Boston: Beacon Books, 1950.

Jameson, Fredric. "Postmodernism and Consumer Culture." In *Anti-Aesthetic: Essays on Postmodern Culture*. Edited by Hal Foster. San Francisco: Bay Press, 1983, pp. 111–25.

Jantsch, Erich. *Design for Evolution: Self Organization and Planning in the Life of Human Systems*. New York: Braziller, 1975.

Johns, David M. "The Relevance of Deep Ecology to the Third World." *Environmental Ethics* 12 (1990): 233–52.

Koestler, Arthur. *The Act of Creation*. London: Huchinson, 1964.

Kuhn, Thomas. *The Essential Tension*. Chicago: University of Chicago Press, 1977.

———. *The Structure of Scientific Revolutions*. Chicago: University of Chicago Press, 1970.

LaChapelle, Dolores. "Systemic Thinking and Deep Ecology." In *Ecological Consciousness: Essays from the Earth Day X Colloquium*. Edited by Robert C. Shultz and J. Donald Hughes. Washington, D.C.: University Press of America, 1981.

Lakatos, I., and A. Musgrave, eds. *Criticism and the Growth of Knowledge*. Cambridge: Cambridge University Press, 1970.

Laplanche, J., and J.-B. Pontalis. *The Language of Psychoanalysis*. Translated by Donald Nicholson-Smith. New York: Norton, 1973.

Laszlo, Ervin. *Introduction to Systems Philosophy: Toward a New Paradigm of Contemporary Thought*. New York: Gordon and Breach, 1972.

Latour, Bruno. "An Interview with Bruno Latour." *Configurations* 2 (1993): 271–92.

———. *We Have Never Been Modern*. Translated by Catherine Porter. Cambridge, Mass.: Harvard University Press, 1993.

Lee, Martha F. *Earth First!: Environmental Apocalypse*. Syracuse, N.Y.: Syracuse University Press, 1995.

Leiss, William. *The Domination of Nature*. Boston: Beacon Press, 1974.

———. *The Limits to Satisfaction*. Toronto: University of Toronto Press, 1976.

Lévi-Strauss, Claude. *Tristes Tropiques*. Translated by John and Doreen Weightnam. New York: Athenium, 1974.

Lingis, Alphonso. *The Community of Those Who Have Nothing in Common*. Baltimore: Johns Hopkins University Press, 1994.

Livingston, John. *The Fallacy of Wildlife Conservation.* Toronto: McClelland and Stewart, 1981.

Lovelock, James. *Gaia: A New Look at Life on Earth.* New York: Oxford University Press, 1979.

Lyotard, Jean-François. *Libidinal Economy.* Translated by Iain Hamilton Grant. Bloomington: Indiana University Press, 1993.

———. *The Postmodern Condition: A Report on Knowledge.* Translated by Geoff Bennington and Brian Massumi. Minneapolis: University of Minnesota Press, 1984.

Manes, Christopher. *Green Rage: Radical Environmentalism and the Unmaking of Civilization.* Boston: Little Brown, 1990.

Margalef, Ramón. *Perspectives in Ecological Theory.* Chicago: University of Chicago Press, 1968.

Mathews, Freya. "Conservation and Self-Realization: A Deep Ecology Perspective." *Environmental Ethics* 10 (1988): 347–55.

McCormick, Bill. "How Deep is Social Ecology." *Kick It Over,* November 1988.

McLaughlin, Andrew. *Regarding Nature: Industrialism and Deep Ecology.* Albany, N.Y.: SUNY Press, 1993.

Merchant, Carolyn, ed. *Key Concepts in Critical Theory: Ecology.* Atlantic Highlands, N.J.: Humanities Press International, 1994.

Merchant, Carolyn. *Radical Ecology: The Search for a Livable World.* New York: Routledge, 1992.

Monaco, Paul. *Modern European Culture and Consciousness.* Albany, N.Y.: SUNY Press, 1983.

Naess, Arne. *Ecology, Community and Lifestyle: Outline of an Ecosophy.* Translated by David Rothenberg. Cambridge: Cambridge University Press, 1989.

Naess, Arne, and George Sessions. "Platform Principles of the Deep Ecology Movement." In *The Deep Ecology Movement: An Introductory Anthology.* Edited by Alan Drengson and Yuichi Inoue. Berkeley, Calif.: North Atlantic Books, 1995.

Nash, Roderick. *Wilderness and the American Mind.* New Haven, Conn.: Yale University Press, 1982.

Odum, E. P. *Ecology and Our Endangered Life-Support Systems.* Sunderland, Mass.: Sinauer Books, 1989.

Oelschlaeger, Max. *The Idea of Wilderness: From Prehistory to the Age of Ecology.* New Haven, Conn.: Yale University Press, 1991.

———. *Postmodern Environmental Ethics*. Edited by Max Oelschlaeger. Albany, N.Y.: SUNY Press, 1995.

———, ed. *The Wilderness Condition: Essays on Environment and Civilization*. Washington D.C.: Island Press, 1992.

Olalquiaga, Celeste. *Megalopolis: Contemporary Cultural Sensibilities*. Minneapolis: University of Minnesota Press, 1992.

Paehlke, Robert. *Environmentalism and the Future of Progressive Politics*. New Haven, Conn.: Yale University Press, 1989.

Rozak, Theodore. *From Sartori to Silicon Valley*. San Francisco: Don't Call it Frisco Press, 1986.

———. *Where the Wasteland Ends*. Garden City, N.Y.: Doubleday, 1972.

Rucker, Rudy, and R. U. Sirius, eds. *Mondo 2000: A User's Guide to the New Edge*. New York: HarperCollins, 1992.

Said, Edward. *Orientalism*. New York: Vintage Books, 1978.

———. "The Text, the World, the Critic." In *Textual Strategies: Perspectives in Post-Structural Criticism*. Edited by Josué V. Harari. Ithaca, N.Y.: Cornell University Press, 1979, pp. 161–88.

Seed, John. "Plumbing Deep Ecology." *Habitat Australia* (June 1982): 27–28.

Seed, John, Joanna Macy, Pat Fleming, and Arne Naess. *Thinking Like a Mountain: Towards a Council of All Beings*. Philadelphia: New Society Publishers, 1988.

Sessions, George, ed. *Deep Ecology in the 21st Century*. Boston: Shambhala Publications, 1994.

———. "The Deep Ecology Movement: A Review." *Environmental Review* 11 (1987): 105–25.

———. "Ecocentrism and the Anthropocentric Detour." *Revision* 13 (1991): 109–15.

———. "Shallow and Deep Ecology: A Review of the Literature." *Ecological Consciousness: Essays from the Earth Day X Colloquium*. Edited by Robert C. Shultz and J. Donald Hughes. Washington, D.C.: University Press of America, 1981.

Shaviro, Steven. *The Doom Patrols*. Online. Available: http://saul2.u.washington.edu: 8080/~shaviro/home.html, 1995.

Shepard, Paul. *Nature and Madness*. San Francisco: Sierra Club Books, 1982.

———. "A Post-Historic Primitivism." In *The Wilderness Condition: Essays on Environment and Civilization.* Edited by Max Oelschlaeger. Washington D.C.: Island Press, 1992, pp. 40–89.

Slicer, Deborah. "Is There an Ecofeminism Deep Ecology 'Debate'?" *Environmental Ethics* 17 (1995): 151–69.

Smith, Mike. "Cheney and the Myth of Postmodernism." In *The Wilderness Condition: Essays on Environment and Civilization.* Edited by Max Oelschlaeger. Washington D.C.: Island Press, 1992, pp. 261–276.

Smuts, J. C. *Holism and Evolution.* London: Macmillan, 1927.

Spigel, Lynn. "Communicating with the Dead: Elvis as Medium." *Camera Obscura* 23 (1990): 177–204.

Sylvan, Richard. "A Critique of Deep Ecology." *Radical Philosophy* 40 (1985): 2–12.

Tansley, A. G. "The Use and Abuse of Vegetational Concepts and Terms." *Ecology* 16 (1935): 284–307.

Taylor, Charles. *The Malaise of Modernity.* Concord, Ont.: Anansi Press, 1991.

Taylor, Mark C. *Altarity.* Chicago: University of Chicago Press, 1987.

Thoreau, Henry David. "Walking." *Harvard Classics,* Volume 28: *Essays English and American.* Edited by Charles W. Elliot. New York: Collier Press, 1910, pp. 407–38.

Tobias, Michael, ed. *Deep Ecology.* San Diego: Avant Books, 1985.

Torgovnick, Marianna. *Gone Primitive: Savage Intellects, Modern Lives.* Chicago: University of Chicago Press, 1990.

Trinh, T. Minh-ha. *Woman, Native, Other: Writing Postcoloniality and Feminism.* Bloomington: Indiana University Press, 1989.

Vattimo, Gianni. "The End of (Hi)story." In *Zeitgeist in Babel: The Postmodernist Controversy.* Edited by Ingeborg Hoesterey. Bloomington: Indiana University Press, 1991, pp. 132–41.

———. *The End of Modernity.* Translated by Jon R. Snyder. Baltimore: Johns Hopkins University Press, 1988.

von Bertalanffy, Ludwig. *General Systems Theory: Foundations, Development, Applications.* New York: Braziller, 1968.

Watson, Scott. "Race, Wilderness, Territory and the Origins of Modern Canadian Landscape Painting." In *Semiotext(e) Canadas.* Edited by Jordan Zinovich. New York: Semiotext(e), 1994, pp. 93–104.

Weed, Elizabeth, ed. *Coming to Terms: Feminism, Theory, Politics.* New York: Routledge, 1989.

Whitehead, Alfred North. *Science and the Modern World*. Cambridge: Cambridge University Press, 1932.

Wilden, Anthony. *System and Structure: Essays in Communication and Exchange*. New York: Tavistock, 1980.

Wittbecker, Alan E. "Deep Anthropology: Ecology and Human Order." *Environmental Ethics* 8 (1986): 261–70.

World Commision on Environment and Development. *Our Common Future*. New York: Oxford University Press, 1987.

Worster, Donald. *Nature's Economy: A History of Ecological Ideas*. Cambridge: Cambridge University Press, 1977.

Zimmerman, Michael. "The Blessing of Otherness." In *The Wilderness Condition: Essays on Environment and Civilization*. Edited by Max Oelschlaeger. Washington D.C.: Island Press, 1992, pp. 263–68.

———. "Introduction to Deep Ecology." *In Context* 22 (1989): 24–28.

———. "Philosophical Reflections on Reform vs. Deep Environmentalism." *The Trumpeter* 3.4 (1986): 12–13.

———. "Rethinking the Heidegger–Deep Ecology Relationship." *Environmental Ethics* 15 (1993): 195–224.

———. "Toward a Heideggerian Ethos for Radical Environmentalism." *Environmental Ethics* 5 (1983): 99–131.

———. *Heidegger's Confrontation with Modernity: Technology, Politics, Art*. Bloomington: Indiana University Press, 1990.

Zizek, Slovoj. *Looking Awry: An Introduction to Jacques Lacan through Popular Culture*. Cambridge, Mass.: MIT Press, 1991.

Index

A
Adorno, Theodor, 64–67, 69
affinity, 124–126
agriculture, 89, 96
anthropocentrism: analysis of, 79–82;
and ecocentrism/biocentrism, 142*n*;
and environmental movement, 35; as
fallacy, 80; and ventriloquism, 81

B
Bateson, Gregory, 56, 57
Baudrillard, Jean, 49, 50, 63, 109
Bentham, Jeremy, 31
Bertalanffy, Ludwig von, 53–56, 57, 60,
75
bio-ideo-colonialism, 76, 78–79
Blade Runner, 134
Blumenberg, Hans, 49
body, the, 104–105
Bookchin, Murray, 26, 28–29, 32–33,
33, 60–61
Border Dialogues (Chambers), 127–130
Bordo, Jonathan, 21–22, 24, 25,
100–101, 158–159*n*, 160*n*
Borradori, Giovanna, 129–130
Boulding, Kenneth, 23
boundaries: analysis of, 106–112; as
constructs, 115; and deep ecology,
105–106; and science and technology,

118, 122; and theory, 127; and
"weak" ecology, 134–135
Bradford, George, 61
Braidotti, Rosi, 106, 125
Bramwell, Anna, 51
Brundtland Commission, 22, 30, 31. *See
also Our Common Future*
Burroughs, William S., 98

C
Canguilhem, Georges, 110, 162*n*
capitalism: and organicist metaphor, 76;
and panopticism, 31; and social
ecology, 32
Capra, F., 60, 67
Carson, Rachel, 17, 20
Chambers, Iain, 127–130
Chaosmosis (Guattari), 122
Chernobyl, 22
Chicago Seven, 26
civilization, Western: renaturalization of,
20
Clastres, Pierre, 43–44, 45, 94, 95, 159*n*
Clifford, James, 75
Closing Circle, The (Commoner), 56
Commoner, Barry, 56, 58, 60, 75, 76
*Community of Those Who Have
Nothing in Common, The* (Lingis),
126–127

Crosby, Christina, 124–125
cultural studies, 5–8
cyberspace, 110
cyborg: and affinity, 124–125; analysis of, 112–115; and boundaries, 106, 124–125, 131–133; as ecological metaphor, 76; and ecological thought, 128; and science fiction, 116–118

D
Darwinism, 21, 94
Davis, Rennie, 26
de Lauretis, Teresa, 114
deep ecology: and anthropocentrism, 100; bias of literature, 94; the body as missing from, 116; and boundaries, 105–106, 111–112; concept of, 33–36; and concept of self, 41; and critical practice, 104; and cyborg, 115; ecosophy T, 143*n*; and Enlightenment ideals, 64, 65; and ethics, 38–39; and fetishized primitive, 121; interpretations of, 39–40; and minority tradition, 42–45; and modernity, 69, 70, 73; and myth, 66–67, 71; and National Socialism, 68; in North America, 39, 45, 147–148*n*; as personal praxis, 41; and perspective, 122–24; platform or principles of, 37–39, 143–144*n*, 144–145*n*; and policies of shallow environmentalism, 40; and the primitive, 94; and primitivist discourses, 95–100; and radical environmentalism, 32; representational practices of, 81, 96–97, 121; and situated knowledges, 123–124; situation of writings about, 37; *versus* "weak" ecology, 135; and wilderness, 82, 100–101, 121. *See also* Naess, Arne; radical environmentalism
Deep Ecology (Devall and Sessions), 39–45
Deleuze, Gilles, 42, 103, 121, 126, 135, 155*n*, 166*n*, 186*n*
Derrida, Jacques, 132–133

Devall, William (Bill), 37, 38, 39–45, 42–45, 81, 95, 96
Dialectic of Enlightenment (Horkheimer and Adorno), 64–67
Doane, Mary Ann, 131–132
Douglas, Mary, 77
Dreamtime: Concerning the Boundary between Wilderness and Civilization (Duerr), 90–92
Drengson, Alan, 39, 71
Duerr, Hans, 90–92, 93, 95, 98, 123

E
earth as closed system, 21
Earth Day, 17, 18–28
Earth Day—The Beginning: A Guide for Survival, 18
Earth First!, 75, 153*n*
ecological self, 81
ecological subject, 104–106
ecological theory, 85
ecological threat: characterization of, 47–48; distinguishing of, 21–22; and ecological discourse, 50; and environmental theory, 79; and humans, 21; and metaphors of disease, 24; representation of, 102; and spaceship metaphor, 23; and "weak" ecology, 135
ecologism, 28–29
ecology: definition of, 47–48, 51; and discourse, 58–63; ecological metaphor, 75–76; ecological science, 61; ecological theory, 48, 49, 58–62; and environmentalism, 48–51; "laws" of, 56, 58; and modernity, 62–64; popular, 48, 55; as prosthesis, 49, 50; relations with science, 48–51; as science, 52, 58; scientific, 48, 55, 59–60; shallow, 34, 40, 47; social, 26, 32–33; and systems, 53–57, 58. *See also* deep ecology; "weak" ecology
Ecology, Community and Lifestyle: Outline of an Ecosophy (Naess), 36–37
Ecology in the 20th Century (Bramwell), 51

ecosophy: definition of, 35; ecosophical thought, 37; and Naess, Arne, 36
ecosystem: definition of, 56–57
Ehrlich, Paul, 20
Enlightenment: analysis of, 64–69; and the body, 104; conception of nature, 32; critique of, 68; and domination, 119; modernism, 120; and modernity, 72, 82; and modes of knowledge, 114; postmodernism, 120; and social ecology, 33
Environmental Action, 18, 138n
environmental movement: contemporary, 17; critical politics of, 27; early, 18, 20; self-representation of, 18–19; as social phenomenon, 28. *See also* deep ecology; ecologism; radical environmentalism, reform environmentalism
environmental theory, 79
environmentalism: and ecology, 58–63; and enlightenment, 66
environmentalism, radical. *See* radical environmentalism
environmentalism, reform. *See* reform environmentalism
ethics: and deep ecology, 38–39; and ecological theory, 60; and ecology, 61; retro-ecological, 69; and "weak" ecology, 134
Evernden, Neil, 58–60, 77–78, 89, 98

F
Fall, the, 89–90
Feyerabend, Paul, 153n
Fitting, Peter, 110–111
Ford Motor Company, 27
Foreman, Dave, 153n
Foucault, Michel, 23–24, 30–31, 105, 135
Fox, Warwick, 35, 39, 41, 79–80, 86
Fuller, Buckminster, 23

G
Gaia, 25
George Sessions, 95, 96

Gibson, William, 110–111, 116, 117, 118
Glacken, Clarence, 84
"God-trick," 25
Goldman, Emma, 33
Goodman, Paul, 33
Grant, George, 71
Grosz, Elizabeth, 97, 161n
Group of Seven, 101
Guattari, Félix, 42, 122, 155n

H
Habermas, Jürgen, 69
Haeckel, Ernst, 51–52
Haraway, Donna, 24–5, 105, 106–110, 111, 112–115, 118–122, 122–26, 128, 129, 131–132
Hardin, Garrett, 20–21, 26, 58
Harding, Sandra, 152n
Hawthorne, Nathaniel, 83
Hayes, Denis, 138n
Heidegger, Martin, 115, 131
Herf, Jeffery, 68, 69
Hölderlin, Friedrich, 115
Horkheimer, Max, 64–67, 69
humans: as actors, 118–120; as apart from nature, 75; as category, 81–82; and ecosystem, 57; erasure of human subject, 79; as exotics, 77, 89, 98; as misfits, 77–78; and move to the outside, 18; as pollution, 77; in radical environmental thought, 33
Humboldt, Alexander von, 51

I
Idea of Wilderness: From Prehistory to the Age of Ecology, The (Oelschlaeger), 84–90, 91–92, 94
image of thought, 4, 138n

J
Jantsch, Eric, 55

K
knowledges, situated, 123–124, 125
Koestler, Arthur, 56

Kropotkin, Peter, 33
Kuhn, Thomas, 70–71

L
LaChapelle, Delores, 39
Laszlo, Ervin, 55
Latour, Bruno, 120, 121, 164–165n
Leiss, William, 27
Leopold, Aldo, 17
Lévi-Strauss, Claude, 57, 132–133
Libidinal Economy (Lyotard), 72
Lingis, Alphonso, 124, 126–127
Lovelock, James, 60, 75, 76
Luke, Tim, 67
Lyotard, Jean-François, 72, 130

M
Magna Mater, 87, 88
Malthus, Reverend Thomas, 20
Marcuse, Herbert, 151n
Margalef, Ramón, 52, 75
marginalized, the, 76, 78–79, 82
Marx, Karl, 32, 141n
Michel, Louise, 33
Minh-ha, Trinh T., 92–93, 101, 127
minority tradition, 42–45
*Modern European Culture and
    Consciousness* (Monaco), 67, 68
modernism, 120
modernity: analysis of, 62–64, 69–73;
    and critical practices, 121; critique of,
    72; and Enlightenment, 69; as
    paradigm, 70–71; and postmodernity,
    131; and science and technology, 122;
    secular character of, 88; and "weak"
    thought, 129, 130
Monaco, Paul, 67, 69
Mondo 2000, 163–164n
move to the outside: analysis of, 17–45;
    and boundaries, 91, 111, 122; and
    carrying capacity, 20–21, 23; as
    category, 19; characterization of, 25;
    construction of "we," 26; and ecology,
    53; and ecosystem, 57; and Enlighten-
    ment, 65; human agency, 38; and the
    marginalized, 82; and modern subject,
    105; position of humans, 75; and the

primal, 43; as response to ecological
    threat, 22, 102
Mumford, Lewis, 33

N
Naess, Arne, 34–39
Nash, Roderick, 82, 83, 84, 93
National Socialism, 68, 69, 73
Natural Alien, The (Evernden), 58–59
Natural History of Selborne, The
    (White), 17
nature: and ecological thought, 77;
    nature/culture, 76, 77, 82
*Nature's Economy: A History of
    Ecological Ideas* (Worster), 93
Neuromancer (Gibson), 110, 118
Nietzsche and Philosophy (Deleuze), 103

O
Odum, Eugene, 52
Oelschlaeger, Max, 70–71, 84–90,
    91–92, 93, 94, 95
Olalquiaga, Celeste, 143n
orientalism, 81, 154n
Our Common Future, 30

P
panopticism, 23–24, 25, 30–31, 134
paratheory, 49–50
Parnet, Claire, 121
phantom limb, 3–4
pollution: commodification of, 28; in
    context of social change, 26; and
    critique of capitalism, 26; economic
    value of, 29–30; and industry and
    business, 27–28; as symptom and
    metaphor, 20
population: carrying capacity, 20–21,
    23; in deep ecology platform or
    principles, 38; Zero Population
    Growth, 20
postmodernism, 119–120
poststructuralism: and identity, 8; and
    structure, 3
Predicament of Culture, The (Clifford),
    75

primitive, the: and boundary zone, 97–98, 101; and ecosystem, 57; and environmental theory, 79; ethnographic claims, 93–94; as idealized figure, 69; and modernity, 94, 98; political dimensions to societies, 94–95; primitivist discourses, 95–100; rhetoric of control, 97–98; rhetoric of desire, 97–98; and ritual practice, 94
psychaesthenia, 143n

R

radical environmentalism: and anthropocentrism, 79; and capitalist practices, 80; critical stance of, 31; critique of, 63; and culture, 77; and cyborg, 113–114; and deep ecology, 39; definition of, 28–29; divisions within movement, 33; and Earth Day, 17; and Enlightenment, 63–69, 71–72; and modernity, 70, 71, 82; and myth, 64; and nature as Other, 78; political topography of, 32; restructuring of, 106; and wilderness, 83. *See also* deep ecology
reform environmentalism: conclusions of, 36; and deep ecology, 35; as deep ecology's Other, 47; definition of, 29–30; as trend within environmental movement, 28
RoboCop, 135
Rothenberg, David, 27
Rozak, Theodore, 59

S

Said, Edward, 154n
Sand County Almanac (Leopold), 17
Scarlet Letter, The (Hawthorne), 83
science fiction, 116–118
Seed, John, 39
Sessions, George, 37, 38, 39–45, 42–45
shallow ecology. *See under* ecology
shallow environmentalism, 79
Shephard, Paul, 75, 95–96
Shifting Paradigms: From Technocrat to Planetary Person (Drengson), 71

Silent Spring (Carson), 17
Smuts, J.C., 150n
Snyder, Gary, 39
social ecology. *See under* ecology
society, Western: and radical environmentalism, 31
spaceship Earth: and ecology, 53; as metaphor, 22–24; and move to the outside, 25
Star Trek: The Next Generation, 116–118
Structure of Scientific Revolutions, The (Kuhn), 70
sustainable development, 30, 31
systems: and ecology, 53–57; General Systems Theory (GST), 53; as metaphor, 21

T

Tansley, Sir Arthur, 57
Tao of Physics (Capra), 67
Taylor, Mark, 62–63
technology: and cyborg, 112; as disaster, 23; as discourse of promise, 23; and ecological crisis, 27; human-machine boundary, 107, 108–110, 117–118; as intervention, 21; and modernity, 68, 70, 122; optimism, 23; technological colonization of earth, 23; technological determinism, 89; and transgression of nature, 78
Thoreau, Henry David, 83, 85, 93
Torgovnick, Marianna, 97–100
Traces on the Rhodian Shore (Glacken), 84

V

Vattimo, Gianni, 72, 128–131
Vietnam War, 27
völkisch movement, 67, 68, 73

W

"weak" ecology, 133–135
"weak" thought, 128–130
White, Gilbert, 17
Whole Earth: metaphor of, 25; rhetoric, 23

Wilden, Anthony, 27, 56, 57
wilderness: analysis of, 83–85; and
  boundary zone, 90–92; Canadian,
  158–159n; characterizations of, 92;
  and civilization, 90; and ecosystem,
  57; and environmental theory, 79; and
  "home," 90; otherness of, 126; as
  secret, 83, 155n

Wilderness and the American Mind
  (Nash), 82, 83, 93
Wilson, E.O., 107
Worster, Donald, 61, 93

Z
Zero Population Growth. *See* population
Zimmerman, Michael, 39